THE

Will You Choose to

GOD

Believe the Impossible?

DARE

Kate Battistelli

PRAISE FOR *THE GOD DARE*

"*The God Dare* will challenge your heart and soul. But more than that, it will encourage you to walk closer with Jesus. And all of us need that!"

—Karen Kingsbury, #1 *New York Times* bestselling author

"Several years ago, God dared me to walk away from all I knew and start my own online company. I didn't call it a dare at the time, but after reading, *The God Dare*, I can see that's exactly what it was. Through her own personal stories and exploring the lives of biblical heroes, Kate will inspire you to discover the path God's chosen for you at this time in history and just where you fit into His cosmic plan."

—Dr. Josh Axe DNM, DC, CNS and author of the bestselling *Keto Diet* and *Eat Dirt*

"Kate Battistelli's new book, *The God Dare*, is filled with practical wisdom and heart-wrenching, personal stories of failure and loss, faith and hope, mistakes and milestones. This book is for anyone who is willing to believe that God can turn your pain into passion, your tragedy into triumph, and take you from mess to messenger."

—Jordan Rubin, *New York Times* bestselling author of *The Maker's Diet* Founder, Garden of Life, Beyond Organic and Ancient Nutrition

"What I love about Kate's stories is how they show that God doesn't just dare us, He also equips us and takes the leap right alongside us! Her testimonies of this truth are a welcome encouragement to those of us who are nervous about putting a toe over the edge of the unknown. This book offers a friend and a God who will both be beside you as you dare to dare."

—Lisa-Jo Baker, bestselling author of *Never Unfriended* and Co-Host of the Out of the Ordinary Podcast

"Frustrated with a complacent walk with Christ? Kate tells us that age, gender, anxiety, past failures, etc. are no excuse for staying where we are. *The God Dare* provides examples of how trustworthy He is—in surprising and supernatural ways! Become a world changer...I dare you...no, God dares you!"

—Pastor Steve Berger, Grace Chapel

"You're braver than you feel, stronger than you know, and loved more than you can even imagine. Kate Battistelli will remind you why all of this is true. She offers the encouragement of a friend, wisdom of a mentor, and contagious courage of someone who has walked with Jesus to places far beyond where she once thought she could go."

—Holley Gerth, *Wall Street Journal* bestselling author of *You're Already Amazing* and *Fiercehearted*

"*The God Dare* teaches us that obedience brings blessings, and that if God has called us, He will also equip us! This book is such a great reminder of what the Bible says in Ecclesiastes 11:4—if we wait for perfect conditions, we will never get anything done. I dare you to read, *The God Dare*, because it will give you the faith you need to take the first step into your God-given destiny."

—Nancy Alcorn, Founder & President of Mercy Multiplied

"We ALL tend to waver when we aren't sure where and what we're being called to. Sometimes the questions seem many and the answers seem few. But if we're being honest, it is often our fear that is holding us back. With personal testimonies of God's faithfulness and encouragement deeply rooted in scripture, *The God Dare* is a stirring invitation to put your trust in the One who has promised to be faithful and walk boldly wherever He leads!"

—Ruth Schwenk, Founder of TheBetterLifeMinistry.com & author of *Settle My Soul*

"With real and raw honesty, *The God Dare* will call you to the radical belief that God wants to use you in His big plans for the world. Kate Battistelli invites you to say YES to God's work in your life, even when it might include a lions' den or a raging sea. You won't find any curated perfection in these pages, only the candid true stories of broken people who, against all odds, decided to take God at His Word."

–Jamie Erickson, author of *Homeschool Bravely: How to Squash Doubt, Trust God, and Teach Your Child with Confidence*

"*The God Dare* is a rare beauty of wisdom and courage, all fortified with God's Word and filled with tested God Dare secrets. Kate has brought back my own dreams, buried once in defeat. *The God Dare* is a gift to the defeated, discouraged, confused, and distracted. Every reader will finish this book, set it down and say, 'Amen. I am here Lord. What's next?'"

–September McCarthy, author of *{Why} Motherhood Matters*, Podcaster @Mom to Mom Podcast and Speaker

"An invitation to the great and wonderfully risky story God is telling, *The God Dare* will nudge you to put feet to your faith. Personally, I was deeply moved and divinely challenged as I read Kate Battistelli's beautifully-rendered book. Take the God Dare; you will never regret it!"

–Allison Allen, author and speaker, books include *Thirsty for More* and *Shine*

"Dares are bold. Triple-dog dares are risky. But a God Dare, the most epic of them all, is life-changing. Kate's wisdom and encouragement pour out on each page of *The God Dare* as she shares God's truth for our lives. More powerful than a 'how-to' book, reading *The God Dare* is like having a mentor sitting right beside you as you navigate the path God created especially for YOU."

–Kristin Schell, author and Founder of *The Turquoise Table*

"Filled with wisdom and grace, *The God Dare* invites the reader on a journey of faith—the kind of faith that trusts in the unseen hand of a faithful God. Kate Battistelli beautifully weaves scripture and stories to guide us as we live out the purpose God has designed for each of us. *The God Dare* is a treasure you'll want to savor."

–Denise J. Hughes, author of *Deeper Waters* and General Editor for CSB (in)courage Devotional Bible

"In *The God Dare*, Kate shares her own journey of spiritual surrender. As you read her story of learning how to trust God, you'll find yourself in the story—whether it's through the taking of giant, future-altering steps of obedience, experiencing heart-breaking losses, the life-long journey of healing from a past failure, or the everyday learning to live like Jesus. Kate lays her heart out to us in hopes that we too will take a sovereign, faithful, merciful God at His Word."

–Katie Orr, Bible teacher, creator of the FOCUSed15 Bible studies, and author of *Secrets of the Happy Soul: Experience the Deep Delight You Were Made for*

"As one who often struggles with fear, I am so grateful to Kate Battistelli for writing this book! *The God Dare* is about saying no to fear and yes to God—yes to His calling, yes to His power, and yes to who He says we are."

–Jennifer Bleakley, author of *JOEY: How a Blind Rescue Horse Helped Others Learn to See*

"Kate Battistelli brings new life to familiar stories of people in the Bible, presenting them parallel to her own experiences. *The God Dare* reminds us that we have the opportunity to 'choose to be chosen.'"

–Anna LeBaron, author of *The Polygamist's Daughter*

"I love the grace-filled challenge Kate Battistelli lays out for us in *The God Dare*—to trust God with our biggest dreams and hopes. It is Word-driven and promising, defying the world's call to self-help. *Yes* to this message, again and again."

—Lisa Whittle, author of *5 Word Prayers*, Ministry Leader, Podcast Host of Jesus Over Everything

"You know what *The God Dare* really is? Because this is much more than a book. It's more like a burning match, lighting a wildfire under your faith. Kate will tell you about her incredible journey with Jesus. But even more, she is inviting you into *yours*—this one wild and beautiful journey that begins with an audacious dare from the One who created you."

—Jennifer Dukes Lee, author of *It's All Under Control* and *The Happiness Dare*

"I remember sitting on the edge of my seat hearing Kate tell her story to a room full of women doing the same. She graciously and boldly invited the women in the room to accept the God Dare. One by one, they did and like me, were changed by it. Let that same invitation to believe God stir your own heart. You will be changed in the best way."

—Stacey Thacker, author of *Fresh Out of Amazing*

"As a friend and mentor, Kate has been encouraging and challenging me to live out the very principles in this book for as long as I have known her. Her passion for walking out *The God Dare* in her own life is contagious. Every word in this book is an invitation, not simply to join her, but to live that overflowing, abundant life God has for each one of us. What a gift Kate and her words are to all of us!"

—Teri Lynne Underwood, author of *Praying for Girls: Asking God for the Things They Need Most*

"*The God Dare* provoked within me a genuine 'yes!' to the invitation of God to live boldly in His calling on my life, no matter what the cost. I was encouraged by Kate's authenticity not only to offer us a peek at her 'mountain top moments,' but her willingness to let us walk into her 'valley moments' as well, so that we can clearly see the faithfulness of God at work in it all and believe Him to be faithful in our own journeys also."

—Francie Winslow, wife, mother of six, speaker

"God dares each one of us to daily pick up our cross and follow Him, so that we can live an extraordinary life for His glory. While this is easier said than done, Kate Battistelli's words will empower you to push fear aside, believe the impossible, and let God transform you as you say yes to every Kingdom dare He puts in front of you."

—Lauren Gaskill, author of *Into the Deep*, speaker, and President of She Found Joy

"In this inspiring book, Kate Battistelli weaves personal, intimate stories from her own life with stories of characters in the Bible who accepted God's Dares. Through Kate's examples, practical application questions, and further scriptures to ponder, each chapter is filled with encouragement to step out of our comfort zones and into God's amazing purposes for us. I finished the book with my own *YES!*"

—Rachel Anne Ridge, author of several books including *Flash the Homeless Donkey Who Taught Me about Life, Faith, and Second Chances*, and her newest release, *Walking with Henry*

"Kate has lived a life of wild obedience and that is evident in the pages of *The God Dare*. She shows us how to do the same and to trust God with our whole hearts even if it looks like we are leaving our dreams behind. Ultimately, saying yes to our God Dare is the pathway to the greatest joy and most fulfilled life."

—Kristin Lemus, Founder of Brave Moms

"Kate Battistelli has thrown down a challenge we don't want to miss. *The God Dare* walks the reader through their own personal step into the Jordan. Whatever that looks like in your story and at this juncture, *The God Dare* has your next steps and a place to process what God is calling you toward for the glory of His Kingdom. Kate puts it best when she reminds us that it's really up to us, but 'It's God's offer to each of us to choose to be chosen.' "

–Shontell Brewer, author of *Missionary Mom*

"In *The God Dare*, Kate Battistelli not only encourages us to take the dares God sends our way, but she also empowers us to say yes by showing us what a God Dare looks like. This book is a wonderful resource to help you place your confidence in God alone and take that first step!"

–Lynn Cowell, speaker and author of *Make Your Move*

"Join Kate as she opens the door for all of us to come in, sit for a while, ignore our excuses, and quiet the shouts of 'should' the world yells at us so we can hear what God is saying. I triple-dog-dare you to possess your possible and choose the narrow path that says no to what the world expects us to do, pursue, and achieve. With *The God Dare*, you'll discover the actual life Jesus has called you to—with less fear and more serving. The impossible is God's comfort zone."

–Crystal Stine, speaker and author of *Holy Hustle: Embracing a Work-Hard, Rest-Well Life*

"There is something special about this book! Power-packed with rich biblical accounts, Kate's compelling story—and an invitation you can't afford to miss—*The God Dare* is for everyone who is ready to leave behind complacent living and respond to God's call to a courageous, faith-filled life. It will be worth it!"

–Katie M. Reid, author of *Made Like Martha: Good News for the Woman Who Gets Things Done*, national speaker, and songwriter

"Through fresh authenticity and passion, Kate Battistelli will inspire and challenge you. She will delight and encourage you with her wisdom. This book breathed new life into my faith. I am undone by Kate's writing and this God who loves and invites us to grand challenges—challenges He fully equips us for."

–Jami Amerine, author of *Stolen Jesus* and *Sacred Ground Sticky Floors*

"*The God Dare* is like a motivational speech in book form. It's your own personal cheerleader in your book bag or purse. The pages will scream out, 'chase that dream' and cast all doubt aside. Kate writes with such passion. Her words give you practical ways to fulfill your own personal God Dare. You will end this book feeling like you can accomplish any task God sets in front of you."

–Lovelle Myers, speaker and contributing author of *A Moment to Breathe: 365 Devotions that Meet You in Your Everyday Mess* and the *(in)courage Devotional Bible*

Foreword by Grammy Award-Winning Artist
FRANCESCA BATTISTELLI

THE

Will You Choose to

GOD

Believe the Impossible?

DARE

Kate Battistelli

SHILOH RUN  PRESS
An Imprint of Barbour Publishing, Inc.

Our mission is to inspire the world with the life-changing message of the Bible.

 Member of the
Evangelical Christian
Publishers Association

DEDICATION

To my incredible husband, Michael. You encouraged me to keep writing this book even when the enemy of my soul did everything he could to stop me. Mike, you are now and always have been my "puzzle part," the one who knows me best and loves me anyway. No one but you and me will ever know how hard we fought to bring this book to life. We paid a deep price, but it was worth every hard day. Thank you for being so much more than I will *ever* deserve.

To my beautiful daughter, Francesca. You are the God Dare in the flesh and you inspire me and everyone who knows you to go a little further, love a little deeper, work a little harder, and be a little braver. Franny, your heart for God and your devotion to your husband and children is an example to us all. I love you with all my heart, and I'm honored God chose *me* to be your mom.

To Eli, Audrey, Isaac, and Wyatt: The four of you give me more joy than you will ever know. I'm excited to see how God dares each of you as you grow. You are here to change the world, and I don't doubt for one second that you will. I am honored to be your "Mimi."

And to our dear friend, June Stone. You never gave up on two jaded New York theatre kids, but you invited us over and over to go to church with you. We finally went and our lives were eternally changed. I shudder to imagine what life would be like today if we'd turned you down. Your faithfulness changed our lives and leaves a legacy we won't fully understand until we get to heaven. We love you!

Then He brought him outside and said, "Look now toward heaven, and count the stars if you are able to number them." And He said to him, "So shall your descendants be." And he believed in the LORD, and He accounted it to him for righteousness.
GENESIS 15:5-6

ACKNOWLEDGMENTS

Thank you to everyone at Barbour Publishing especially Kelly, Shalyn, Faith, and Liesl for all your hard work on my behalf!

A big thank-you to my agent Jessica Kirkland of Kirkland Media Management. You fought hard for *The God Dare* from the beginning and went above and beyond to get it out in the world. Thank you for believing in me and my message.

Thank you to all my Hope*Writer friends for your encouragement and prayers along the way.

Also, a big thank-you to Lona Fraser and all the members of Heartprint Writer's Group from my church, Grace Chapel in Franklin, Tennessee. You guys let me read almost every word of this book to you over the last two years, and you offered wonderful encouragement and advice that I took to heart. Thank you for being excellent midwives!

Thank you to my dear friend Maureen Eha. You are the first one who encouraged me that my blog post called "The God Dare" could be a book. I knew you were right, and this book is the result. Thank you, sweet friend, we've known each other for decades and been through all the ups and downs together. *The God Dare* owes its existence to you.

Father God, we've walked together for thirty-five years and You continue to love me, deal gently with me, encourage me and surprise me. Since I don't believe in retirement, I look forward to all the ways You will dare me in the years ahead! I love You most of all.

CONTENTS

FOREWORD

I've come to learn that most scary things are really only scary the first time. Of course, there are exceptions (ain't nobody gonna pay me to go on another rollercoaster), but most of the things we're scared to try are things that will make us stronger, happier, better versions of ourselves. They are the things that will change our lives and the lives of others.

I remember when my mom first told me the title of her new book. It was years ago, but I knew then that it would be special. I knew it would change lives because I knew she had a story to tell. A story of walking the walk—of taking the God Dare again and again in so many ways all her life. She always taught me to "do it afraid." Whatever it was—a ballet audition, telling a friend about Jesus at school, playing my guitar for the first time in front of an audience, moving across the country to Nashville to follow a dream—I heard her voice in my head saying, *You can do this.*

In this amazing gift you're holding in your hands, she lays her soul bare. She lets us in on her past—the good, the bad, and the broken—and she gives us a simple choice: will we take God at His word or not? As I read these pages, I remembered the countless times we sat together, coffee in hand, talking about these epic stories and heroes from God's Word and how they all had one thing in common—they were not afraid to take the God Dare.

So what stops us so often from taking the God Dare? Several things, I'm sure, but at their core, I believe the answer is fear. Fear—that small seed of doubt that can turn into a tidal wave of paralyzing dread. The enemy uses it against us constantly, and it's time we recognize it for what it is: an act.

You see, the enemy can't create anything; he can only twist what's real. He's so good at it, though, that we often misinterpret it as truth. Except any thought that doesn't come from Jesus is a lie, so if the voice you're hearing tells you "You are not good enough," the truth is exactly the opposite: "You are worthy." If the lie is, "You can't do (fill in the blank)," the truth is "You can do all things through Christ who gives you strength." We must learn to walk in the opposite spirit. We must learn to take the God Dare—the dare to simply believe the truth about who we are as children of God.

What if we started this journey with open hands and an open heart? With a prayer that goes something like, "Lord, help me identify the lies that the enemy has been speaking to me, so that I can come out of agreement with them and can clearly hear what You say about me. As I read, let Your truth wash over me. Let Your Word cleanse me from the lies I've been believing. Let this be the beginning of a wildly beautiful adventure with You. Wherever You want to take me, I am Yours!"

So, what about you, friend? Are you ready to go adventuring with Jesus? Are you ready to let Him decide what is best for your life? Remember that your thoughts are not His thoughts.

Your timetable is not His timetable. Your plans are not nearly as fantastic as His are for you. I encourage you to open your hands and let go of what's holding you back, or what you're holding on to, so that He can take you somewhere you've never dreamed. I encourage you to take the God Dare!

–Francesca Battistelli Goodwin

Introduction

What's the crazy dream God has dropped in your heart? The wild adventure He's inviting you to join? What is He asking you to do that you know you couldn't possibly do on your own? In fact, if you try to do it on your own you're pretty much guaranteed to fall flat on your face? Has He given you a wild, preposterous, secret, scary, or enchanting dream or idea? That's what I call a God Dare. Because with God *anything* is possible.

I bet that's why you picked up this book. I have a feeling you've been sensing it for a while now. It might wake you up in the night or come out of nowhere as a random thought you know didn't come from your brain. Or it called to you in a dream or you sensed it some other way. But as soon as you sensed it (if you're anything like me) the excuses flooded in:

> "Who am I?" you ask. "I'm not equipped."
> "What can I possibly do to change the world? It's not in me."
> "I've messed up way too much. God couldn't possibly use me."
> "I'm too old. There's no way. I missed my chance."
> "I'm too young. I don't understand any of this."
> "God doesn't even know I exist. Why would He use *me*?"
> "I'm too tired."

. . .and a million other excuses, fears, and insecurities we use to excuse ourselves from God's divine nudge.

A God Dare is simple, really. It's God's *yes*. His gigantic smile and nod of the head, His holy high five beckoning you to believe. Begging you to take Him at His word, and to once and for all let go of fear, doubt, guilt, and pride, and say yes to *His* yes. It's God's offer to each of us *to choose to be chosen*—to say *yes* to His magnificent plan for your life. Your part is to trust Him and step into the unknown place He's been asking you to consider for some time. . .maybe years. But fear and doubt have stopped you.

The God Dare Is Trusting That God Will Equip You to Accomplish What He's Called You to Do

Could God be daring you to keep holding on to that long-held dream you barely recall? Is He daring you to let go of that false view of yourself you've believed far too long? Perhaps He's daring you to step out in faith and do something completely impossible and outside your comfort zone. But you can take this truth to the bank: the impossible *is* God's comfort zone.

What is God daring you to do? It likely won't look like you think it should. It *will* cause you to trust Him in a way you haven't before. Know this: when the God of the universe dares you to follow Him into the bottomless ocean of trust, He'll equip you with everything you need. He is well aware you can't *begin* to accomplish a God Dare without His help.

Let me be honest and tell you up front, friend: this is a book about faith. Big faith, pure faith, reluctant faith, miraculous faith, risky faith, relentless faith, crazy dangerous faith, biblical faith—but ultimately the unseen faith that comes from one source only: God. If you want a sure thing, you don't want a God Dare, because all trust and all faith requires risk. It requires believing in something you cannot see.

When the "Not Yet" Becomes the "Will Be"

Faith is actual substance and true evidence, but you can neither see nor touch it; you can only apprehend it. Faith knows beyond the shadow of a doubt that over time the "not yet" turns into the "will be." It's the tangible assurance that what we're hoping for will really and truly come to pass.

Our lack of faith quenches the supernatural. It has the audacity to deny God's character, power, and ability to do what He says He will do. Honestly, it's much easier to live your life with no faith. Life without faith is undemanding, unexceptional, complacent, and comfortable but undeniably stodgy and boring. And those living that way end up exiting this world exactly as they entered it. Surprisingly, few are willing to sacrifice the good in order to attain the best. But God invites each and every one of us to believe and to walk by faith. However, there's a caveat He reveals in His Word: "Let us hold fast the confession of our hope without wavering, for he who promised is faithful." (Hebrews 10:23 ESV).

It's *our* choice whether or not we will choose to be chosen. It's *our* choice to risk everything in order to change the world.

The God Dare is a perspective shift, a realization that God created you, yes *you*, for a divine reason. You're not some random clump of cells casually dropped onto this planet. No. You're on this planet for a reason, and maybe you haven't figured that reason out yet, but I'm hopeful this book will help you do just that.

No matter who you are, how old you are, what you've done, or what's been done *to* you, you are not disqualified. You are here *on* purpose and *for* a purpose. You might not know what that purpose is yet (Moses didn't know till he was eighty), but that doesn't matter. What matters, and what I hope you glean as you keep reading, is that you are on God's mind. You can't begin to number the thoughts He thinks toward you. God calls you His masterpiece, His poem, His treasured possession. The God of the universe has His eye on *you*.

You might be thinking, *You don't know what I've done*, or *I have a checkered past and I've done things I'm ashamed of,* or *I don't deserve anything good.* I can promise you this: *my* past is so checkered you could play chess with it and still have pieces left over! I don't deserve a single thing I've been given. But that's the cool thing about God. He sees us according to our destiny, not our history. He never lets our past hinder our future if we've repented and asked for forgiveness. He still forgives, and He still heals, and I'll make it crystal clear as you keep reading.

When Jesus called the disciples, He didn't beg, plead, or cajole. As He walked the dusty road, He merely said, "Follow Me." Following was *their* choice. It was up to *them* whether they would choose to follow, choose to obey. What does a God Dare feel like? *Like a cosmic bungee jump into God's fascinating, incredible, and world-changing future.*

I think we have it all wrong. We search desperately for the very thing pursuing *us.* We search, we dig, we look. We fret and question, wonder and worry, and all along it's right there in front of us, right under our noses.

Can you smell the intoxicating fragrance, seductive in its beauty, frightening and overwhelming your senses with power and possibility. . .drawing you, reminding you of something you used to believe but have forgotten somewhere along the way? The God Dare surrounds us, pregnant in our every day, infusing profound purpose into each moment small or large, ordinary or awesome.

The God Dare will challenge you to go further than you believed possible. It will cause you to take God at His word, to believe and obey, to say yes even when the yes might cost you. God is looking for world-changers, the ones willing to fling it all out on Him in one gigantic leap of faith. All He asks in return is for you to trust Him to the end. I promise you, His dreams for you are bigger than you could ever imagine!

I won't sugarcoat it. Taking a God Dare can be hard and full of doubt and difficulty, but at the same time its world-transforming power is miraculous and saturated with wonder! You're called to this because you are worth it, my friend.

If you're anything like me, you may not feel equipped to change the world *at all*. I've come a long way in my walk with the Lord after thirty-five years, but you know what? I still have a long way to go. I've wrestled with fear like nobody's business. Just in the last few years I've experienced crippling anxiety and then seizures that hit me out of nowhere. I've been crabby and critical, jealous and easily offended. I've even thought my ideas and agenda were more important than anyone else's in my world. If you don't believe me, just ask my husband.

I've wrongly believed my ways, my wants, my wounds, and my worries were the most important of all. I've been reluctant to accept how the God of the universe sees me. I've failed miserably and given in to the lie that I'm not important to God. . .that my story doesn't matter. I've failed way more than once.

I've not been brave lately. And I desperately want to be brave. I don't like to fly, I won't go on roller coasters, I wouldn't be caught dead bungee jumping. But I'm asking God to make me brave, to make me fear-LESS. Do you track with me? I'm a wimp and a chicken, and I'm over it. The Bible doesn't say we will never fear, but it does tell us how to fight when fear attacks: "Whenever I am afraid, I will trust in You" (Psalm 56:3).

Maybe you've failed and been afraid too. Maybe you think you've missed His purpose for your life or you've blown it too badly to ever be forgiven or used by God. Trust me, you haven't. God will use *anyone* (even a donkey) if they're willing to be used.

I want to be open and transparent with my life so you don't have any preconceived notions about me. I've had some amazing experiences and triumphs, but the ugly truth is I've dealt with impatience, self-pity, addiction to antidepressants, jealousy, anxiety, pride, and more. *Much* more.

God is not surprised by my capabilities *or* my many weaknesses. Just today I was crabby and impatient with bad drivers on the road, and I might have used one of those words that is *not* in the Bible. Yet as I trust God and walk into His purposes for my life, He grows my confidence and strengthens my faith. I'm coming to realize God still seeks the ones who will say yes even when it makes no sense, even when others will doubt you ever heard God, even when you feel unworthy, and even when saying yes will cost you.

I believe God gives each of us handpicked opportunities to choose to be used by Him to accomplish His holy purposes on the earth. Our free will allows us to say no if we want to, and sadly many of us—no, *most of us*—do. But imagine the possibilities when we say yes!

What does a God Dare look like? I see God daring folks all through the Bible. He might dare you to move away from your homeland like Abraham. Or He might ask you to risk your life in a hostile land to spread the Gospel like Jonah. Or maybe you'll be raised up as a great leader like Moses or Joseph or given favor and an exalted position to save your nation like Esther—or offered an opportunity to obey God in a thousand and one ways you *can't begin* to imagine.

God radically dares each of us every single day to humble ourselves, to forgive those who've harmed or offended us, to live generously, to pray for our enemies, to love the unlovable without judgment or offense, to wash another's dirty feet, and so much more. What if God dares you to give up your right to yourself, to turn the other cheek, to be defrauded, to walk the second mile, to be reconciled to your brother? He actually dares us to *live* according to what we read in the Bible. My friend, you can *"wash your face"* or, you can wash someone's feet.

The God Dare Is for Those Who Are Willing to Choose to Be Chosen to Make the Impossible Possible

I promise you, when God dares you to step out, the stepping won't be easy and it will cause you to question *everything* you think you know. But here's the thing: world-changers don't always know they're changing the world. Do you think Joseph, the beautiful dreamer, imagined he would one day become the number-two leader in all of Egypt, providing the nation of Israel a home to thrive and grow and multiply? I can't imagine Ruth (a pagan) or Rahab (a pagan prostitute) ever looked at their lives and assumed one day they would worship the God of the Israelites and find themselves in the lineage of Jesus Christ. When God called Esther to risk her life to present her petition to the king, there is no way she could have known her actions would save her nation from extinction.

Those willing to take a God Dare risk their lives, hide spies, kill giants, cast out demons, paint blood on doorposts, speak truth to power, touch the hem of His garment, waste costly ointment, stretch out their withered hand, lower friends through roofs, follow when they don't know where they'll end up, and obey what they might not fully understand. *The ones who take a God Dare fearlessly live out their faith.*

The God Dare will catch you off guard, shaking up everything you *think* you know about your future. Yet when you say yes, you'll suddenly find yourself positioned to change the world. When you say yes to the possible, watch God do the impossible.

The God Dare in its simplest form is knowing deep down inside that you're on this bedraggled planet for a reason. You're not simply taking up space, but God has a specific plan in mind *just for you*. In fact, He chose you for it before the foundation of the world. He designed you very specifically for this time and this place, and He will perfectly equip you to accomplish His purpose on the earth. Your job is to choose. It's the inkling, the drawing, the knowing that gnaws. . .that's the God Dare!

We'll figure out this God Dare stuff together. Each chapter will include several relevant scriptures to ponder, discussion questions for yourself or a small group, and the many God Dare secrets I've learned over the years.

The God Dare is trusting that God will equip you to accomplish what He's called you to do.

The God Dare is God's offer to each of us to choose to be chosen.

The God Dare is a cosmic bungee jump into His fascinating, world-changing future.

The God Dare is realizing God created you for a reason.

The God Dare is doing it afraid.

Chapter 1

MY FIRST GOD DARE

The first time I heard the God Dare, it didn't have a name. I only knew this: I was heading one way, and God dared me and my husband to go in the *complete opposite* direction.

My husband, Mike, and I had gotten married just a couple of years earlier and at the time, we lived in a 720-square-foot condo in trendy Greenwich Village in Manhattan. Both of us were pursuing promising careers in the Broadway musical theater world—Mike as a conductor and musical director on Broadway and Radio City Music Hall and me as an aspiring Broadway actress and singer.

We'd met a couple of years earlier, in 1981, on the national tour of *The King and I* when I costarred opposite Yul Brynner. I'll share more of our story later, but I was blessed to perform as the leading lady on tour and Mike acted as associate conductor. . .and we really and truly fell in love across the footlights.

Two years earlier we'd become devout Christians, and a year later I gave birth to our daughter, Francesca. As we grew in our relationship with the Lord, an uneasy feeling about our chosen professions began to well up in us both, as the music and theater worlds are not typically known as God-honoring industries. I found it increasingly necessary to turn down auditions for morally questionable projects, and my theatrical agents were none too happy about it. I realize now God allowed deep testing in our lives by bringing sizable opportunities for fame and fortune to see where our hearts truly resided. Would we choose the narrow path? Would we follow our Good Shepherd? Would we lay down the life we loved?

I remember receiving an offer from a producer in South Africa to come and perform in *The King and I* for several months. And I'd just found out I was pregnant. He wanted to pay me a lot of money, but apartheid was at its height and I knew there was no way I was going to South Africa. He kept calling and sweetening the deal, but even with all his flattery, I stood firm, knowing there was no way, morally, I could go. Not to mention being pregnant. . .and wearing hoop skirts!

A rising and uncomfortable sense about our life choices continued to creep in. One rainy night as Mike and I watched a preacher on Christian TV, we felt as if he suddenly pointed right at us through the screen, saying something about "you actors and musicians who think you can live a hypocritical life. . .God is telling you to lay down your careers and *come out from among them*!" Whoa, Nelly, now that got our attention!

I don't typically make life-altering decisions based on what I see on television, but the TV preacher merely confirmed what Mike and I already sensed. The Broadway theater world, the lights, the fame, the backstage glow and glamour of New York City, no longer felt like home. Ultimately, we listened to that still, small voice nudging at our hearts and decided to make a major ninety-degree lifestyle shift.

I do believe many are called to the arts and the theater. However, as baby Christians, God knew our hearts and likely also knew temptation and compromise would rear their ugly heads. Our first God Dare required us to completely walk away from the music and theater worlds and lay down our hopes and dreams for fame and fortune.

Let me assure you, giving up your lifetime dream is no picnic. My husband and I worked *years* to bring our dreams to life, and now God, who we barely knew, asked us to trust Him and leave our dreams in the dust. It felt incredibly strange since our entire identities were wrapped up in our careers. My husband has a doctorate in conducting for Pete's sake! How do you just walk away from *that*? We'd been utterly convinced our lives were destined for the Broadway theater. But God had a better plan, even though we couldn't quite see it at the time.

Walking away from everything familiar (like Abraham) is one of the most difficult God Dares but, ultimately, one of the most rewarding. If you sense God calling you to a different path than the one you are currently on, let me give you hope that it's for a bigger purpose than you can possibly know right now. I'm intimately acquainted with how difficult it is, but just know, the years *will* give the perspective you lack now. I promise.

For some of you reading this, He may be calling you *into* the theater world or the arts. I pray He will give you discernment and wisdom as to whether He wants you to shine His light in the darkness. The arts have grown incredibly bleak over the last few decades, and they desperately need strong believers to shine the light of truth!

Ninety-Degree Turns

God loves to challenge us with what I call "ninety-degree turns" in this life—the opportunity to go in a completely different direction—even when it makes no sense to the rest of the world. Of course, our theater friends thought we were crazy by walking away from established and growing careers. Had we stayed in our careers, I'm confident we would have continued to do well and experienced an even greater measure of success. But even as young and immature Christians, we knew there was only one viable choice for us—we *would* pick up our cross and follow.

We prayed about it, sought good counsel, and ended up buying a pretty little house in a small town outside Princeton, New Jersey, not far from where we'd grown up (and still only forty-five minutes from Broadway!). We took God's crazy dare and laid down the glitz and glamour of New York City for a home business and homeschooling, taking God's ninety-degree turn and utterly altering the paths of our lives.

I'm quite certain God knew (even if we didn't) as we laid down our dreams in obedience to follow Him that He planned to pick those dreams back up in the next generation through our daughter, Francesca. In fact, as the years went on we were blessed to witness just how much *our ceiling would become her floor*.

God's economy is never wasteful, and He never wastes the training and experiences He gives you. When our daughter, Francesca (Franny), began expressing her gifts and talents in music, we were able, because of our backgrounds, to help her navigate the music world, instill in her the value of hard work and diligence, and remind her she could change the world with the gifts God had given her. Obeying God's leading by laying down our careers became our first God Dare.

When the "Not Yet" Becomes the "Will Be"

Faith is the substance of things hoped for,
the evidence of things not seen.
HEBREWS 11:1

Let's take a quick look at Abraham. We'll take a deeper dive into his life in a few chapters, but for now let's just take a quick glance. At the advanced age of seventy-five, Abraham receives instructions from *God Himself* to walk away from everything he knows—his familiar country, his thriving business, his family, his father's house—and follow God to a land He would show him.

Abraham's free will allowed him to either say no to God or take the plunge and choose to follow. Of course, we know the outcome. And because of his faith, God granted Abraham incredible promises including making him a great nation, making his name great, and that in him all the families of the earth would be blessed—all because he made the bold choice to trust and believe God, stepping out with Him into an uncharted and impossible-to-know future. Abraham was willing and prepared to do *anything* for God. What about you?

The silken thread connecting so many biblical heroes is this: God dropped in their laps the divine opportunity to choose to be chosen. Each of them could have turned God down, and I'm certain He would have offered the chance to change the world to someone who would say yes.

We like to think we know God's plan for our lives, don't we? I imagine Peter the apostle, dripping wet after a long day at sea on his creaky boat, or maybe mending old, worn nets in the harbor as he hears a voice calling him to "Follow Me." Perhaps Peter thought he had his life all figured out as he fished each day in the Sea of Galilee. I doubt in his wildest dreams he ever imagined he would walk away from a thriving business to follow a man he knew precious little about. Yet Peter must have sensed *something* extraordinary in the One who called him to follow that day, because ultimately he *did* walk away from everything familiar, leaving nets and boat behind, and in choosing to follow Christ, Peter ended up being chosen to change the world.

Self-righteous Paul certainly wasn't looking for Jesus. In fact, Paul had no problem allowing Christ's disciples to be murdered, chasing them down and persecuting those who followed The Way. One afternoon he traveled the dusty road to Damascus with a single focus: bring the followers of Christ bound to Jerusalem. Suddenly a heavenly light surrounded him, and he found himself knocked down on his blessed assurance, completely blind. Jesus Christ Himself offered Paul the divine opportunity to lay down everything he thought he knew and preach the Gospel to the

Gentiles. Paul, in choosing to follow Christ, wrote the majority of the New Testament, became a revered martyr for his faith, and utterly changed the world.

Will You Let Jesus Pick?

I had a fascinating dream recently. I was with some young generation X ladies my daughter's age, and we were talking and catching up. In the dream, one young lady told me about her recent marriage and how it was distinctly different from what the glitzy bridal magazines had led her to believe. Another gal, well into her thirties and still unmarried but desperate for a husband and children, shared her deep loneliness. As we talked, I knew in my dream I wanted to pray for them and share my heart and the perspective that comes with age. So I began to pray for the girl who wanted what most young women want—marriage and kids—and as I prayed in the dream, I sensed God say these remarkable words to me: *"She wants a husband and sons, but what she doesn't know is I want to give her a nation."*

I was stunned, absolutely *stunned* by His remark. I'm not sure what God meant by that statement, but as I woke up, this realization hit me like a ton of bricks: He wants so much more for us than we can ever begin to dream up. We think we know what we want—it's what we're supposed to want, right? Doesn't our culture teach marriage and parenthood are our highest goals? They're absolutely worthy goals, but are they God's will for every person on the planet? *God's love can be frightening in the freedom it provides.*

Hmmm. Maybe we set our sights too low. Do we want what the world romanticizes because we don't set our sights on *Him*? Because we don't want Him *enough*? Don't we know the only thing in this world ever able to truly satisfy our deepest heart longing is *Him*?

We prove we don't know by whining, complaining, regretting, seeking everything to satisfy us *but* Him. I wanted so badly to ask her in my dream, *What if God asked you to lay down your desires and risk your future on Him? Would you trust Him enough? What if He didn't have a husband and family for you but instead something entirely different yet completely wonderful you didn't plan on? Would you take Him at His word? What if God dares you to walk a narrow path, one that flies in the face of everything our culture says you should want; do you love Him enough to walk the unique path He chooses for you? Do you love Him enough to let Jesus pick?*

I'm believing that if you're reading this book, you're hungry for His will, for purpose, for destiny. What do we all desire? Significance. Living a life that matters. Leaving behind a legacy leading others to the truth.

Look at your dreams. They're good and righteous, I'm sure. But maybe, just maybe, He has a different path in mind for you, precious one. Maybe your God Dare doesn't look like you think it should. Don't forget, He created you before the foundation of the world, and He knows exactly where He wants to take you. It might look different than you think. In fact, *He might want to give you a nation.*

Scriptures to Think About

- *"Blessed is that servant whom his master will find so doing when he comes."* (Matthew 24:46 ESV)
- *Now the LORD had said to Abram: "Get out of your country, from your family and from your father's house, to a land that I will show you. I will make you a great nation; I will bless you and make your name great; and you shall be a blessing. I will bless those who bless you, and I will curse him who curses you; and in you all the families of the earth shall be blessed."* (Genesis 12:1–3)
- *"For I know the plans I have for you,"* declares the LORD, *"plans to prosper you and not to harm you, plans to give you hope and a future."* (Jeremiah 29:11 NIV)

- *Now faith is the substance of things hoped for, the evidence of things not seen.* (Hebrews 11:1)
- *"Many are called, but few are chosen."* (Matthew 22:14)

God Dare Secrets

- If He calls you to it, He knows you can accomplish it. . .not in your strength but in His. You will have to step out and reach out for the help you need, but He'll provide every element at the proper time.
- God wants more for you than you could ever dream up.
- Most people won't take the God Dare because it can be uncomfortable, and in the Western world, we value comfort above all. As a result, most will ignore that still, small voice.
- There is an enemy called "average." Each one of us has exactly what it takes to be average. Being average, remaining under the radar, and not making waves is *exactly* where the enemy wants to keep us.
- God's economy is never wasteful, and He doesn't waste the training He gives you.
- Sometimes your ceiling can become another's floor.
- God's love is frightening in the freedom it provides.
- We choose whether or not to be chosen.
- Our lack of faith quenches the supernatural.
- Few are willing to sacrifice the good to attain the best.

Discussion Questions

- What would your life look like if you took God at His word and believed you had world-changing potential?

- Do you believe you have the capacity to change the world?

- Do you believe there's a God Dare designed just for you? What do you think it is?

- Are you willing to venture outside your comfort zone and bungee jump into your future?

- Are you willing to sacrifice the good to attain the best? What will that require?

- What kind of legacy do you want to leave behind?

- Will you choose to be chosen? If not, why not?

- If God offers you a ninety-degree turn, will you take it?

- What's stopping you from taking your God Dare?

- Will you let Jesus pick?

Chapter 2

MY SECOND GOD DARE

I heard it clear as a bell several years ago. My husband, Mike, and I were invited to speak at a meeting in Orlando, Florida, for the large homeschooling organization we'd been part of for many years. They began planning a giant blowout for their twentieth anniversary, and because we'd homeschooled Francesca with them, they asked us to share with the attendees the steps we'd taken to raise her into a woman of God who had found her purpose and was living out her destiny. By this point in her life, she'd signed her record deal and she'd had number-one hits on the radio. They asked us to speak about what intentional steps we'd taken as her parents to put her on the path to purpose.

At first I panicked and thought, what the heck *did* we do? Maybe we were just super lucky? But as Mike and I talked it over, we realized we'd been *very* intentional in the actions we'd implemented to raise our daughter to pursue her destiny with passion and purpose. So as we talked it through, we came up with fifteen concrete steps we'd followed in our parenting. I dutifully wrote out our steps, and later that week Mike and I spoke at the meeting.

The morning after the meeting, I stretched out on the carpet to worship, pray, and thank God for allowing us to share our talk and the fifteen steps we'd taken, and for all of God's blessings in our family. I was awash in gratitude for the opportunity to connect with other families and share our story as I went over in my mind the fifteen topics we'd discussed the night before.

And that's when I heard it, the God Dare. Or what I like to call

God's big, fat, triple-dog dare. Here's what I heard God speak deep in my spirit: *"Those are book chapters."*

Wait, what? Book chapters? Are you *serious*, God? You want me to write *a book*?

No way, God, I can't. And here's why:

1. I'm not a trained writer.
2. I don't have a college degree.
3. I'm not a parenting expert.
4. I don't have time to write a book. (I knew that wasn't true, but I thought it anyway.)
5. Who will read it?
6. How will I ever get it published?
7. People will think it's a stupid idea.
8. People will think I'm promoting myself.

And on and on and on. . .

The sentence exploded in my brain like a firecracker, and though I went into hyper-mode desperately searching for an excuse not to listen to His crazy words, I couldn't find one. I *had* no excuse. It's funny, all the things I'd taught my daughter about how to cross self-imposed boundaries, step out of your comfort zone, and how to do it even when you're afraid—they all flooded in to haunt me in that moment.

I reminded God I was *not* a writer, I had no platform, no college degree, no way to get a book published, and on and on. I gave God every excuse I could *think* of, and you know what He told me, over and over as His answer to every excuse I could come up with? *"Those are book chapters."*

So I did the only thing I could. I said yes to God's triple-dog dare. I chose to believe He knows me better than I know myself, and He knows *exactly* what I'm able to accomplish, and if I say yes, His part in the bargain is to equip me to carry it out. In that moment, I made one unalterable and life-changing decision: *I would choose to be chosen.*

Over the next year I found a writing coach, and I blew through every single one of my excuses by the act of *doing* what He dared me to do, which was to write a book. I actually did, and my first book, *Growing Great Kids*, was published in January 2012!

If He Calls You, He'll Equip You

Get this: I found a publisher who was eager to take my book when I had no serious writing experience, no platform, and no college degree. (I actually went to four colleges in two years and didn't graduate from *any* of them, but that's another story.) So don't give me any excuses about why you can't do something. If God calls you, anything is possible. *Anything.* If He calls you *to* it, He'll equip you to *do* it.

The truth is, I knew I had a choice. I could have chosen to limit myself and ignore the still, small voice, to settle for less, to stay safe and stuck in my comfort zone, but I'm so glad I didn't. I'm glad I pushed through my excuses, and I'm proud of the book I wrote! And now I can officially call myself by a new name: *writer and author*.

Think about this. Moses took the God Dare. I imagine him in the back of a hot, steamy desert leading stinky sheep for forty years . . .years full of solitary, sweaty days and cold, starry nights, likely imagining he'd completely missed his purpose. Then suddenly a bush on fire in the distance catches his eye. He could have chosen to ignore the bush, maybe thinking he was seeing a mirage, but he didn't. Instead, he said, " 'I will now turn aside and see this great sight, why the bush does not burn.' So when the LORD saw that he turned aside to look, God called to him" (Exodus 3:3–4).

And God dared him. Here's my *very* loose paraphrase: "Hey,

Moses, you've been leading sheep for forty years. I've chosen you to lead human sheep for another forty out of bondage and oppression and into a land flowing with milk and honey. They will pretty much drive you nuts for four decades, but *you're My guy*."

We all know how the story ends. Moses takes the dare (with great reluctance), and with his brother Aaron's assistance he completely alters history and brings about the birth of the nation of Israel.

What about Abraham? "Hey there, Abraham, you're a hundred years old and your wife is ninety and you're both way past childbearing age, but in spite of that I'm giving you more descendants than the sand on the seashore or the stars in the sky. In you all the families of the earth will be blessed. Trust Me." And he did, *and we are*.

Or Ruth. "Hey, Ruth, I want you to move away from everything you know and follow your sad, bitter mother-in-law to her country where you have absolutely no prospects. I know it looks hopeless, and it makes no sense, but trust Me." And Ruth, a heathen non-Israelite, obeyed and ended up in the lineage of Christ.

Don't forget teenaged Mary, who took the most incredible God Dare of them all. Eight simple words of hers forever changed the world, "Be it unto me according to thy word." (Luke 1:38 KJV). And the rest is history. . . .

All these biblical heroes, and so many more, simply took God at His word when they chose to trust and invest in hope and faith; and God didn't let them down. It wasn't easy for any of them, and each of them paid a price. But their obedience and examples of faith continue to change lives today.

What about you? Will *you* take the God Dare? What's He daring you to do? Maybe He wants you to go back to school or start a business in the inner city, or adopt a baby from a crack-addicted mother, or begin a ministry to the homeless, or move across the world to be a missionary in a perilous country hostile to the Gospel. Maybe He's inviting you to write a book or a screenplay. Perhaps He's calling you to live quietly in your community, serving like Christ in the day-to-day by loving your neighbors, raising your children, and changing your world in the small sphere. Maybe you're called to politics or medicine or the arts, and it's going to take years of training to bring your God Dare to pass. Maybe you'll have to fight for your dream. But isn't anything God calls you to worth fighting for?

Are you willing to wake up, look around, open your ears to hear what God is saying to you, and grab ahold of the bungee cord and . . .*JUMP*?

I triple-dog dare you. Take the God Dare. I hate to be the one to tell you, but we don't get an "opt-out clause" if we call ourselves Christians.

Friend, I'm here to help. In these pages, I'll provide concrete examples from the Bible and real life to help you on your journey. We'll talk about the devil's dare and its devastating consequences and the many enemies of every God Dare. I'll share specific ways to bring the God Dare to pass in your own life and some of the hindrances you may (okay, *will*) encounter. And last, we'll discuss the greatest God Dare of all.

One thing I can guarantee: if you take God at His word, trust Him and step out, you *will* be changed and you *will* change your world.

Stick with me as you ponder your own triple-dog dare!

Scriptures to Think About

- *"I will now turn aside and see this great sight, why the bush does not burn." So when the LORD saw that he turned aside to look, God called to him.* (Exodus 3:3–4)
- *Be it unto me according to thy word.* (Luke 1:38 KJV)

- *The counsel of the LORD stands forever, the plans of his heart to all generations.* (Psalm 33:11 ESV)
- *For the LORD is good; His mercy is everlasting, and His truth endures to all generations.* (Psalm 100:5)

God Dare Secrets

- In taking the God Dare, God transforms us into the men and women of God He created us to be.
- God is future-minded and thinks generationally. What you do or do not do will impact the world throughout history.
- When we take the God Dare, our obedience changes the world.
- If He calls you *to* it, He will equip you to *do* it.
- To believe the impossible, we must see the invisible.
- You can ask God for an extra measure of faith.
- When you take the God Dare, you can call yourself by another name.

Discussion Questions

- Have you ever felt God dare you to something bigger than you felt qualified to accomplish?

- How did it make you feel? What did you do about it?

- What is God daring *you* to do?

- How can you know if your dreams line up with God's desire for your life?

Chapter 3

THE PATRIARCH

Mike and I sensed it at the exact same moment. We'd been married a couple years and had our baby girl, and there we were listening to that TV preacher and feeling deep conviction about our lives and chosen professions. At the time we lived in New York City's West Village as we pursued burgeoning careers in the Broadway Musical Theater world.

We met a few years earlier on the national tour of *The King and I* where I had my first big role starring as Anna opposite movie star Yul Brynner (maybe you've seen him as Pharaoh in the movie *The Ten Commandments* or as the original king in the movie *The King and I*). We toured the nation for almost three years, and I performed the role more than one thousand times, knowing beyond the shadow of a doubt that theater and music were what we were destined to do for the rest of our lives. (I'll share more of our story in chapter 5.)

But soon after we were married, we experienced a life-changing encounter with Jesus. And before long, He asked us to turn our lives upside down and lay aside everything we *thought* we wanted and walk with Him into a *very* different world.

We'd gotten married in July 1983, and we gave our hearts to the Lord in March 1984 in an all-black church in Jamaica, Queens, New York. Our dear friend June, a born-again Jewish lady, invited us to go to church with her for a number of months. We kept politely turning her down. Eventually though, we got to the point where it would have been downright rude to say no one more time. So when she invited us to go with her on a Friday night because "*you will love the music*" (and we did), we succumbed and said a reluctant yes. We had no idea what to expect or what kind of church we were heading to as we rode the F train to the last stop in Jamaica, Queens, on that Friday, March 31, in 1984.

It turned out we were heading to a "holiness church" in an old, converted movie theater. We had no idea what that meant at the time. When we arrived, the men sat on one side and the women on the other, and all the women wore modest skirts or dresses and no makeup or flashy jewelry. And worn crutches and braces and old wheelchairs covered the lobby, all from folks who'd apparently been healed. Being raised in an extremely liturgical Episcopal church, I felt like I'd been dropped by parachute onto a foreign planet or at least entered a foreign country. I had no touchstone for the exuberant worship of a God I didn't really know. Singing the staid doxology was as exuberant as my church ever got! But the Holy Spirit moved and breathed in this place, and with deep joy our hands shot up in the air when the pastor gave the invitation to be saved that night.

Some months later, Mike and I looked at each other with confusion and at the same time, deep certainty. Questions and hot tears flowed as we talked it through, and the more we talked the more we knew. We were going to walk away from budding careers, the beginning of fame, and the hope of great fortune. Our friends and my theatrical agents would think we were nuts, but we knew beyond the shadow of a doubt we made the right decision.

Our daughter entered the world that next year, and we were confident New York City was not the place we wanted to raise our family. In obedience, but with more tears and trepidation, we sold our condo in Greenwich Village and moved to a quaint country town near Princeton, New Jersey, trading everything we knew— our friends and the life we loved, music and the footlights, fame and fortune, New York pizza and Zabar's everything bagels—for a new life. It made no sense at the time, and our theater friends and colleagues were convinced we had lost our minds. . .but we knew. *We knew.* And obedience would be the key to our future. It was the key to Abraham's future too.

Have you ever wondered how Abraham mustered the courage to leave everything behind when God first called him? How did he find the strength to walk away from his pleasant, comfortable, and familiar life, forsaking everything familiar—home, friends, and family—when God asked him to risk it all and go to a new place He would *show* him? Would Abraham trust completely and step out of the boat?

We often think of biblical icons like they're presented in the movies. We imagine Moses as Charlton Heston with his flowing white beard, his staff and robes, or Abraham resembling craggy Richard Harris. Some of us might imagine Mary, the mother of Jesus, with a glowing halo around her head as she tenderly cradles the baby Jesus. I'm convinced those images couldn't be further from reality. The characters we meet in the Bible were humans just like us, with all of humanity's faults, foibles, and failings, and Abraham is no exception. He had many admirable qualities, it's true. But Abraham also blatantly lied—and asked his wife to lie for him—he partially obeyed God, and he failed more than once. The enemy loves to hide in our blind spot. . .and we most often never even see him coming. Nevertheless, Abraham's obedience and humility completely changed history.

Somehow Abraham discovered a precious secret, what I like to call "*The magic of risking everything for a dream that nobody sees but you.*"[1] I love how Abraham actually responded when God asked him to. He rose up and left everything he'd ever known to follow God's prompting. I love that about him, don't you? Trust me, it's not easy when God dares you to "Get out of your country, from

---

[1] From the film *Million Dollar Baby* (Warner Brothers, 2004).

your family and from your father's house, **to a land that I will show you**. I will make you a great nation; I will bless you and make your name great; and you shall be a blessing. I will bless those who bless you, and I will curse him who curses you; and in you all the families of the earth shall be blessed" (Genesis 12:1–3, emphasis added).

God told Abraham what to do and why. . .but not *how*. Abraham, one of the ancient wanderers born just five generations after the scattering that occurred at the tower of Babel, didn't know where he was being led. . .but he intimately came to know the One who led him. He was a businessman being asked to do something that made no sense. In an era of polytheism and perverse idol worship, Abraham began a personal relationship with a God who, up until that time, he knew nothing about. Abraham didn't obey God perfectly, and his partial obedience led to much trouble later on. Yet God's promises came to pass *in spite of* Abraham's failures. Abraham obeyed God's leading to leave Haran, and he traded his known present for an unknown future: "He went out, not knowing whither he went" (Hebrews 11:8 KJV).

The Space between the Going and the Showing

Notice God said, "a land that I will show you." God didn't say a land I will *tell* you about. No. He just asked Abraham to go *and in the going would come the showing*. Although Abraham had no idea where he was going, and God asked him to follow blindly, he did! Can you even imagine? From what I can see, Abraham did it for one reason: "Abraham 'believed God'" (Galatians 3:6).

Those are three of the most radical words in all of scripture. *He believed God.* Abraham took God at His word. He trusted God meant what He said, so he said yes to God's prompting. He didn't argue or equivocate. The Bible never says he prayed about it, talked to his best friend, sought counsel, put out a fleece, or even discussed it with Sarah. Abraham simply trusted and said yes. He radically, though imperfectly, believed God. Abraham said yes because he had faith enough to risk everything to follow a God he had never known and walk smack-dab into the unknown. Abraham is the God Dare in the flesh.

However, Abraham only partially obeyed. When God instructed him to **"Get out of your country,** from your family and from your father's house, **to a land that I will show you"** (emphasis added), Abraham chose to bring along his aged father (who died shortly after) and his nephew Lot. They parked themselves in Haran after God had already told him to leave, which led to much trouble later on. The whole Lot/Sodom and Gomorrah issue could have been completely avoided had Abraham fully obeyed God and left Lot in Haran. Partial obedience *always* has consequences.

Can you imagine if we believed God when He spoke to us? I don't know if you're anything like me, but I pretty much always tell God no first. I see all the obstacles, all the difficulties, all the things that can go wrong, and I let fear have its reign. Oh, how I wish I could be more like Abraham, to hear God out and not analyze or overthink it to death. When we're willing to let God help Himself to our misbegotten lives, there's no telling *where* we'll end up. It can be a scary place, the place in between, the space between the going and the showing. But it's there where we learn to trust. And I won't kid you, it's not an easy place, not an easy place at all.

I'm amazed at the way God revealed to Abraham what was to come. God promised Abraham if he would forsake the familiar place of family and home and step out in crazy obedience, God would make him a great nation. He would bless him and make him famous, and whoever blessed Abraham would be blessed and whoever cursed him would be cursed, *in spite of* his imperfections and partial obedience.

What about Sarah? God's promise to Abraham didn't mention Sarah at first. It wasn't until twenty-five years later that Sarah received her promise. Little did she know, God began laying the groundwork for laughter to mark her life in a way she could never begin to imagine. The promise and the continuation of the covenant would come through *her*. Her son, Isaac, whose name means "laughter," came to her in spite of her shortcomings and her futile efforts to bring God's promise to pass in her own strength.

God took time to teach Abraham how to think bigger than he ever had before. He told Abraham to look at the vast land and walk around in it as He helped him visualize his future. I imagine God saying, "Look at it, Abraham, walk around in it, touch the dirt, smell the breeze, feel the warm sun on your skin and see it with your own eyes. Imagine your own children living here and growing and thriving. Then believe it's really and truly for you."

> *The Lord said to Abram after Lot had parted from him,*
> *"Look around from where you are, to the north and south,*
> *to the east and west. All the land that you see I will give to*
> *you and your offspring forever. I will make your offspring like*
> *the dust of the earth, so that if anyone could count the dust,*
> *then your offspring could be counted. Go, walk through the*
> *length and breadth of the land, for I am giving it to you."*
> (Genesis 13:14–17 NIV)

Now, mind you, this is decades before Abraham has any children. He's known as Abram when he receives this promise, and he's seventy-five years old. The Bible tells us Abram was extremely wealthy in livestock, silver, and gold, and had 318 trained servants, basically a small army of fighting men. His wife Sarai is sixty-five and barren. . .her deepest desire for a son having never come true. Talk about your impossible dream! It's what I call one of God's big, fat, triple-dog dares! You do *this*, Abram, and I'll do *that*. Now comes Abram's second God Dare:

After these things **the word of the LORD** *came to Abram in a vision, saying, "Do not be afraid, Abram. I am your shield, your exceedingly great reward." But Abram said, "Lord GOD, what will You give me, seeing I go childless, and the heir of my house is Eliezer of Damascus?" Then Abram said, "Look, You have given me no offspring; indeed one born in my house is my heir! And behold, the word of the LORD came to him, saying,* **"This one shall not be your heir, but one who will come from your own body shall be your heir." Then He brought him outside and said, "Look now toward heaven, and count the stars if you are able to number them." And He said to him, "So shall your descendants be." And he believed in the LORD, and He accounted it to him for righteousness.** (Genesis 15:1–6, emphasis added)

God promised a multitude of descendants, and Abram believed God would do it. He lifted his head to gaze at the starry sky glittering with more twinkling stars than he could ever count, and in that moment made a bold choice to believe in the impossible. This marks the first time in all of scripture that "the word of the LORD" comes to a person—and it comes with a covenant. God wants us to take Him at His word. Most of us won't, but Abram's heart was willing, and because of that, God gave him a new name and fulfilled *every single one* of His promises.

Abram could have said no. He could have told God he was quite comfortable and happy right where he was, thank you very much. He could have chosen to stay safe in Haran and walk away from a future destined to change the world. And if he did, I'm quite certain God would have found someone else, someone with the capacity to see what doesn't yet exist. Someone who "calls those things which do not exist as though they did" (Romans 4:17).

One night, God tells childless Abram to number his

descendants by going outside and counting the stars, an impossible task—and God gives Abram a brand-new identity. Abram's God Dare happened on a starry night thousands of years ago, and because Abram took the God Dare and believed, God counted him righteous, having already given him this amazing promise: "And in you all the families of the earth shall be blessed" (Genesis 12:3).

Thanks be to God for all our sakes that our dear, aged Abraham risked it all, grasped ahold of an impossible future, and *believed*. In spite of his imperfections, Abraham is my Old Testament role model. He was likely set in his ways and probably just wanted to settle down and enjoy the childless years he had left. But here comes God with talk of sand and stars and making this man who has no heir a great nation, and He would bless all the families of the earth through him. What in the world? What would *you* do if God brought that kind of promise to you?

God called out Abram's deepest dream and promised to do the impossible. And Abram, simple Abram, simply believes. I always want to maintain that same childlike faith and take God at His word even when it makes absolutely *no* sense to my carnal mind. To remember that even though I can't see the end from the beginning, *God can*.

God held a big, God-sized dare with Abraham's name on it, just waiting for him to grab hold of the bungee cord and take the first step off the ledge. Abraham, by believing God had a future for him, took that first step, and in the stepping it all fell into place. It wasn't easy, and it took decades to fully come to pass (which is often the case with the God Dare), and it didn't come without Abraham and Sarah first making a huge ugly mess of it. But in spite of it all, *every dream of Abraham's came to pass.*

Abraham and Sarah had incredible faith. Yet, like all of us, their faith and obedience were inadequate. Abraham asked his wife to lie for him more than once. His misunderstanding of God's promise caused him to father a child, Ishmael, with Sarah's maid Hagar, and the Ishmaelites are still at odds with Israel today. (Sarah shows what happens when you take God's promises into your own hands—*the outcome will never be good.*)

Even though the Lord told Abraham to leave his family behind, he brought Lot along when he left Haran, which led to major strife between his herdsmen and Lot's. After they separated, Lot headed to wicked Sodom and Gomorrah, and then, after some time and because of the great depravity there, God eventually destroyed Sodom and Gomorrah, Lot's wife turned into a pillar of salt, and Lot's daughters got him drunk and committed incest with their own father. From that unsavory episode, we got the Ammonites and the Moabites, who became Israel's arch enemies. Nevertheless, Abraham believed God's promises. He kept plowing ahead and he continued to trust God would do the impossible. How many of us let our past failures keep us from moving into the future with God? Remember this: God's faithfulness will always outlast our failure.

There's one more lesson Abraham can teach us about the God Dare. Sometimes God will ask us to lay down the very dream He's promised us, the heart cry He's dared us to believe in. Because sometimes even a good dream can become an idol. Here are wise words from A. W. Tozer:

The baby represented everything sacred to his father's heart: the promises of God, the covenants, the hopes of the years and the long messianic dream. As he watched him grow from babyhood to young manhood the heart of the old man was knit closer and closer with the life of his son, till at last the relationship bordered upon the perilous. It was then that God stepped in to save both father and son from the consequences of an uncleansed love. "Take now thy son," said God to Abraham, "thine only son Isaac, whom thou lovest, and get thee into the land of Moriah; and offer him there for a burnt-offering upon one of the mountains which I will tell you."[2]

Years after the promised son, Isaac, arrived, God dared Abraham a third time. He dared him to sacrifice his precious son as a burnt offering, the son of the promise he'd waited twenty-five years to come to pass. God had substantially proven Himself to Abraham, and because of his history with God, Abraham didn't question or rage or cry or complain. He had such an incredible level of faith. "Abraham figured that if God wanted to, he could raise the dead" (Hebrews 11:19 MSG).

Abraham simply obeyed when God spoke. There's a huge lesson here: never, *ever* let your God Dare consume you, and never let it become an idol. Obey quickly in everything. "Abraham rose up early in the morning" (Genesis 22:3 KJV).

Scriptures to Think About

- *Abraham believed God and it was accounted to him for righteousness.* (Galatians 3:6 KJV)
- *Now the LORD had said to Abram, "Get out of your country, from your family and from your father's house, to a land that I will show you. I will make you a great nation; I will bless you and make your name great; and you shall be a blessing. I will bless those who bless you, and I will curse him who curses you; and in you all the families of the earth shall be blessed."* (Genesis 12:1–3)
- *Who, contrary to hope, in hope believed, so that he became the father of many nations, according to what was spoken, "So shall your descendants be." And not being weak in faith, he*

---

[2] A. W. Tozer, *The Pursuit of God* (n.p.: A. W. Tozer Books, 1948), 32.

did not consider his own body, already dead (since he was about a hundred years old), and the deadness of Sarah's womb. He did not waver at the promise of God through unbelief, but was strengthened in faith, giving glory to God. (Romans 4:18–20)

- *God, who gives life to the dead and calls those things which do not exist as though they did.* (Romans 4:17)

- *The righteous shall flourish like a palm tree, he shall grow like a cedar in Lebanon. Those who are planted in the house of the LORD shall flourish in the courts of our God. They shall still bear fruit in old age; they shall be fresh and flourishing, to declare that the LORD is upright; He is my rock, and there is no unrighteousness in Him.* (Psalm 92:12–15)

- *He went out, not knowing whither he went.* (Hebrews 11:8 KJV)

God Dare Secrets

- When God dares us, He calls out our deepest dreams and the desires of our hearts.

- God Dare–takers must trust He has a plan. As God calls out our deepest dreams and we face our deepest fears and say yes, just watch Him do the impossible. Just watch Him prove that we are indeed fearfully and wonderfully made for such a time as this.

- The God Dare is a spiritual bungee jump. You risk everything. You jump and trust the cord will hold!

- Never let your God Dare become an idol.

- God's faithfulness will always outlast your failure.

- It's tempting to create Ishmaels and call them Isaacs.

- When we give God permission to help Himself to our lives, *there will be fruit.*

- Abraham didn't know where he was being led, but he knew the One who was leading him.

- The unknown is where world-changing adventures happen.

Discussion Questions

- Have you ever found yourself in the scary, in-between place, the place between the going and the showing? What did it feel like to be there?

- When was the last time you radically obeyed God?

- Have you decided you're either too young or too old to take the God Dare? Why?

- Are you willing to risk it all for a dream nobody sees but you? What if you don't?

- Will you trade your known present for an unknown future if God asks you to?

- Will you radically obey God even if others think you're crazy?

- What would it look like if God had permission to help Himself to your life?

- Will you choose to be chosen or will you shrink back?

- Are you willing to embrace the future God has for you even if it's different from what you planned?

Chapter 4

THE ADULTERESS

I turned eighteen the summer I found out I was pregnant. It was 1972, and I'd just graduated from high school and I knew quite well that in my family, an out-of-wedlock pregnancy simply wouldn't do. If I'd told my overly critical and easily annoyed mother about it, I'm quite certain she would have marched me directly to the nearest Planned Parenthood for an abortion. The terror of her finding out about my condition prevented me from ever telling a single family member. *Ever.* The thought of both distressing her and incurring her wrath, and knowing full well my father's deep disappointment if he found out, frightened me more than any other choice I had. I already walked on eggshells trying to please parents with impracticable standards no one could measure up to.

In fact, besides my husband and a tiny handful of friends, I've never publicly shared this story. The shame and guilt still cause hot tears to overwhelm even now, more than forty years later. It's something that just doesn't go away no matter how old you are or how "good" a Christian you may think you are or appear to be to others. The shame and guilt stay with you, and if left alone, fester deep in the pit of your soul. It's the one truth about me I've had the hardest time revealing because, like everyone, I want folks to think well of me. I want my daughter to think well of me. I want my neighbors and pastor and Bible study companions to think well of me. I want you, my reader, to think well of me. I want you to think my Instagram profile is the full truth of my life, but, just like yours, *it's not.* I carefully curate the life I want you to believe I'm living.

At least until today, when I've decided it's time to get honest with my ugly.

I knew in late May of that year, deep in the pit of my stomach, something was amiss. I didn't have my monthly visitor and I chalked it up to just a fluke. But it didn't visit in June or July either. By August, I finally admitted to myself what might be going on, and with trepidation, I discussed it with the long-haired, rock-'n'-roll-playing young man who was my boyfriend during those years. He blithely suggested I go to Planned Parenthood, which was about the only option I could see, so I agreed and went. The pregnancy test was confirmed and my worst nightmare came true.

I remember how the woman in charge coldly asked me if I wanted to have the baby. Of course I was horrified and said NO! I was a teenager for goodness' sake! What would my family think of me? How would I ever get rid of the giant scarlet letter that would be tattooed forever on my forehead? If I had a baby, how would I ever live my dream of singing and acting. . .how would I become a Broadway star? I was already on thin ice in my family because of this particular boyfriend, since he was a few years older, dropped out of high school, and, horror of horrors, played guitar in a rock band.

To say I was rebellious at that age is an epic understatement. My upbringing was decidedly upper middle class, and some things simply weren't done. Except *I did them*. As the often overlooked middle child, I'd learned to play the game well. My manners at the country club were impeccable. I knew which fork to use, not to lick my fingers, how to fold my napkin in my lap, and how to make a lovely appetizer tray (and my mother's *very* stiff gin martinis). But my rebellious behavior out of the sight of my parents had become, well, let's just say, far from admirable. I hated everything my parents stood for, and I did all I could behind the scenes to break every one of their taboos. Like getting pregnant and not going to college.

Like smoking pot and moving in with my boyfriend. Like breaking their hearts over and over again.

I told the woman at Planned Parenthood I couldn't possibly have a baby, and she told me I would have to go to New York in order to get an abortion. I lived in New Jersey then, where abortion was still illegal in 1972 as *Roe v. Wade* had not yet become law, but abortion was legal in New York. So she gave me the information of a doctor in Manhattan and set up the appointment for me.

My boyfriend drove me into Manhattan on that warm, regrettable September day. I was terrified, confused, and conflicted but resolute in my decision. I could visualize my future but *not* with a child. . .and I couldn't imagine how having a baby at eighteen would improve my life in any possible way. I honestly believed I had no other option, and no one at any time counseled me or let me know there were alternatives like adoption available to me. Fear made my decision for me because I could see absolutely *no way* to solve what felt like a gigantic invasion of my life and body.

I remember a kind nurse helping me that day as she prepped me for the procedure. I took off my clothes, put on the flimsy gown, and laid down on the cold table with my legs spread-eagled in the stirrups. When the doctor came in the room, he turned on the big, noisy machine and began the abortion. He let me know in his soft French accent I was right on the cusp of four months and if I'd waited even one more week he wouldn't have been able to do the grisly procedure. I felt incredibly grateful he could, having no idea that by the end of the fourth month your tiny baby is about six inches long and weighs about four ounces. The nervous system is well developed at that point, and doctors can tell if you're having a boy or a girl.

Naturally, they didn't share any of those facts with me at the time. I have no idea whether it would have changed my mind though. To be completely honest, I imagine I would have gone ahead anyway. Fear of my parents' reaction stopped me cold and moved me to a decision I will *forever* regret. I've always sensed it was a baby boy, but I won't know for sure until I get to heaven.

After the abortion, which was the vacuum aspiration kind, the kind that sucks the tiny fetus out in bloody pieces, I remember getting dressed. Instantly the thought popped into my head, *You're a murderer.* I did my best to ignore the awful truth of what had just happened, and I justified my decision. Hey, it was my body, the women's liberation movement told me. And I succeeded in this justification for a number of years. . .at least until I met the Lord a dozen years later and was reminded God knew exactly what I had done. . .and loved me anyway.

I've kept my secret well hidden for decades because of the traumatizing fear of being labeled a fraud, and I've wrestled like mad over even *writing* this chapter and having it in my book. Putting my story out there is my most recent, difficult, and terrifying God Dare. But, you know what? *I'm done with fear.*

I'm done with guilt and shame. I'm *done*, and I'm over letting the enemy of my soul keep me from sharing my ugly truth, because I want others to know that with Jesus, He can and He does make all things new, and He truly and forever forgives us when we ask Him to. He changes our name and He changes our future when we allow our heart to come to grips with our deformed and broken truth. When we give God our sin, He gives us salvation. He still gives *His* beauty for *our* ashes. . .and He still does more than merely heal the broken. He uses them.

I may not have committed the sin of adultery, but I've always felt a kinship with the unnamed woman caught in adultery and used as a pawn to accuse Jesus, a broken woman heartlessly dragged out to the murderous crowd and smugly accused before the Son of God.

Oh, how I love the way He loves women so well. In case you

haven't read the story in a while, here it is. It's short but powerful, and there's an incredible God Dare, or should I say, Jesus Dare at the end:

> *Now early in the morning He came again into the temple, and all the people came to Him; and He sat down and taught them. Then the scribes and Pharisees brought to Him a woman caught in adultery. And when they had set her in the midst, they said to Him, "Teacher, this woman was caught in adultery, in the very act. Now Moses, in the law, commanded us that such should be stoned. But what do You say?" This they said, testing Him, that they might have something of which to accuse Him.* **But Jesus stooped down and wrote on the ground with His finger, as though He did not hear.**
>
> *So when they continued asking Him, He raised Himself up and said to them, "He who is without sin among you, let him throw a stone at her first."* **And again He stooped down and wrote on the ground.** *Then those who heard it, being convicted by their conscience, went out one by one, beginning with the oldest even to the last. And Jesus was left alone, and the woman standing in the midst. When Jesus had raised Himself up and saw no one but the woman, He said to her, "Woman, where are those accusers of yours? Has no one condemned you?"*
>
> *She said, "No one, Lord."*
>
> *And Jesus said to her, "Neither do I condemn you;* **go and sin no more.**" (John 8:2–11, emphasis added)

I've always wondered what Jesus wrote on the dusty ground, right in front of the self-righteous Pharisees, the accusers, and the unfortunate woman who had obviously been set up just so they could have an opportunity to slander Jesus' character. Scholars think He wrote the names of the accusers and what sins deserving of death they had each committed. That makes sense, and it could very well be. But I wonder if He wrote something about *her*. Maybe He scratched *her name* in the dust and true words describing her future. What if He addressed her sin life but also her soul's worth? What if He wrote words like:

> *Forgiven*
> *Beautiful*
> *New creation*
> *Chosen*
> *Fearfully and wonderfully made*
> *Child of the King*
> *Bride*

What if He let her read those dusty words as He sent her on her way? He's said these words about me. They are the only reason I can even *begin* to take God's scary dare and share my story with you in this chapter. I am a new creation, and I am forgiven. So are you, my friend. No matter what you've done, said, caused, believed, you *are* forgiven if you ask Him to forgive you. If you take Jesus' life-changing dare to go and sin no more, to believe you are on this planet for a reason and your life matters. Are you aware Jesus is praying for you? He knows all your faults and sins, and He loves you and is praying for you anyway. Guilt and grace are fighting for the same place in your life. Let go of the guilt and give in to His marvelous, life-changing grace.

Our past will affect our future, but it doesn't have to determine it. No matter how badly you've messed up, God can and will use you if you're willing to be used. *No circumstance has the final word over you.*

To accept forgiveness and release shame and guilt is one of the most difficult God Dares of all but one of the most critical if we're ever going to move forward with God. If I can receive forgiveness for my abortion, you can receive forgiveness for whatever you've done. It's not too late. Sometimes you need to clear off all the china and reset the table of your life. If you're reading this and you're still breathing, it's not too late. Just do the thing. If God can take rebellious me and transform me into His bride, He can do it for you too. Stop playing footsy with sin. Ask Him, press in, repent of your sin, and let His love wash over you and make you new. It really does work, and it really is true. It's the God Dare that will change eternity and make you forever His. My cover is blown now. What about yours?

Scriptures to Think About

- *"Therefore, behold, I will allure her, will bring her into the wilderness, and speak comfort to her. I will give her her vineyards from there, and the Valley of Achor as a door of hope; she shall sing there, as in the days of her youth, as in the day when she came up from the land of Egypt."* (Hosea 2:14–15)

- *"Has no one condemned you?" She said, "No one, Lord." And Jesus said to her, "Neither do I condemn you; go and sin no more."* (John 8:10–11)

- *Let no one say when he is tempted, "I am tempted by God"; for God cannot be tempted by evil, nor does He Himself tempt anyone. But each one is tempted when he is drawn away by his own desires and enticed. Then, when desire has conceived, it gives birth to sin; and sin, when it is full-grown, brings forth death.* (James 1:13–15)

- *If we confess our sins, he is faithful and just and will forgive us our sins and purify us from all unrighteousness.* (1 John 1:9 NIV)

- *As far as the east is from the west, so far has he removed our transgressions from us.* (Psalm 103:12 NIV)

God Dare Secrets

- You can be bruised and brave at the same time.
- God both heals and uses the broken.
- God's Word and His promise are one.
- Guilt and grace are fighting for the same place in your life.
- Let your fear face God.
- He still forgives sin, and He will forgive yours if you ask Him to.
- Jesus knows all your faults and sins and is praying for you anyway.

Questions to Think About

- Do you have a hidden sin you've never shared with anyone? Are you willing to?

- Are you willing to, once and for all, release all fear, guilt, and shame? What will change if you do? What will happen if you don't?

- Do you have the courage to let your cover be blown?

- Do you know what words He's written about you?

- Do you have any idea how much He loves you in spite of what you've done?

Chapter 5

THE QUEEN

When I toured with *The King and I* back in the early 1980s, I wasn't a Christian and I had no idea God had such a quirky sense of humor! Little did I realize then that God was about to use my current life as a prophetic picture of His future for me. I was a mere twenty-six years old at the time.

I was cast in the Broadway national tour of *The King and I* as the understudy for Anna, the "I" in the title. I knew my job as understudy served primarily as an insurance policy for the show's producers. Never in a million years did I think I'd get a shot at playing the lead role with the famous and very imposing Yul Brynner. So I dutifully did my job in the chorus. God invited me to dance with Him in obscurity, in the chorus, as the understudy. God the Father began calling me even then, giving me a prophetic picture of what my life could be if I chose to dance with *Him.*

I never dreamed I'd come into the theater at 7:15 one night to find the leading lady out with pneumonia and that I had to go on and "whistle a happy tune" in forty-five minutes! Remember this was back in 1981, decades before cell phones and computers. I'd been out all day shopping with friends and had no way of knowing I was performing that night.

When I arrived at the theater, the nervous stage manager grabbed hold of my shoulders, looked me straight in the eyes, and said, "She's sick. You're on!" I didn't have a second to freak out (or back out!). He brought me to the leading lady's sumptuous dressing room, and her hairstylist and wardrobe assistant attended to me as they prepared me for the show. I nervously put on my makeup, desperately trying to wrap my mind around the responsibility laid in my lap just moments before.

I'd had lots of understudy rehearsals so I knew my role backward and forward, but I'd never worn a single costume (or the enormous hoop skirts that are *heavy*!), handled a prop, or performed a scene with Yul Brynner who was a *huge*, iconic star in those days. If you've ever seen the movie *The Ten Commandments* he played Pharaoh, not to mention he starred as the original king on Broadway *and* in the movie version of *The King and I*. Yikes!

To say I was intimidated is a massive understatement, but I had no time to do anything but anxiously prepare and battle the fear deep in the pit of my stomach. About fifteen minutes before the curtain rose, the king summoned me into his elegantly appointed dressing room to speak with me. Yul Brynner always wore all black, even down to his underwear. As I entered his dressing room, the king sat ensconced in front of his mirror, painting on his eyebrows for the show wearing *only* his black underwear. Imagine my intimidation! Of course I was terrified, but his kindness and encouragement got me through that night, although I can't remember *what* he said to me.

I went out and performed the entire three-hour show completely terrified, rushing so quickly through it, I cut fifteen minutes off the run of the show! (Sometimes you just have to *do it afraid*.) But I finished the show in one piece and ended up going on for the leading lady for another two weeks. When she returned to the show, I dutifully went back to my place in the chorus, because that's just what you do when you're an understudy.

But the story doesn't end there. Over the next couple of weeks, the king decided he liked performing the show with *me*. He and the leading lady didn't really get along, and apparently both were unhappy working with the other. So, even though he could have his choice of dozens of New York actresses to choose from, the king chose *me* to replace her. Not only did he choose me, he bought out her entire two-year contract so he could put me in this bigger-than-life role of a lifetime!

Let me tell you, friend, in the theater world that just doesn't happen. But, incredible as it sounds, it did for me. The king reached down and lifted me up out of the chorus and made me the leading lady in one of the greatest female roles in all of musical theater history. And I was a mere twenty-six! Back then it was *The King and I*. But today? It's the KING and i. I just love God's sense of humor, don't you?

Spiritual Bungee Jumps

What's a spiritual bungee jump? It's when you risk everything you have—your future, your comfort, your agenda, sometimes your very life—to step into God's divine destiny, a destiny handpicked for you. It's the mother of all God Dares because it takes great faith *and* great courage. The Bible makes this promise in Romans 12:3 to those who are in Christ: God "has dealt to each one a measure of faith."

Each of us has at least as much faith as a mustard seed. But few of us take the risk and ask God for great faith because we know, if we've walked with God for any length of time, our faith *will* be tested.

How else can you grow in faith unless God allows something in your life you have to have faith *for*? Faith only becomes real when it's tested. How can you believe God is who He says He is unless He allows situations that cause you to stretch and grow and see Him as more than just a great big blessing machine in the sky?

Spiritual bungee jumps are reserved for those willing to lay down their lives for something bigger than themselves. For those who "loved not their lives even unto death" (Revelation 12:11 ESV).

Esther faced death in order to bring freedom to her people.

We are all here for a reason at this exact time in history and in this precise place. "And He has made from one blood every nation of men to dwell on all the face of the earth, and has determined their preappointed times and the boundaries of their dwellings" (Acts 17:26).

Each of us are part of God's divine plan, and some have assignments more visible than others. All assignments are important, but some of them rewrite history. Esther received one of *those* assignments.

Don't you just love Esther? An ordinary girl who won the genetic lottery and was blessed with great beauty. Plucked from obscurity (like David, Joseph, Moses, Mary, Gideon, etc.), God handed Esther position and honor to bring salvation to an entire people group. She showed such courage, reluctantly at the outset, but really who wouldn't first count the cost? She dug deep and found the ability to step into a role she never asked for, allowing herself to be used by God even at the risk of becoming a martyr for her faith. Esther gives us all a marvelous example of enormous courage and trust as she eventually realized her life was not her own. Here's her story.

A beautiful Jewish orphan, Esther, whose name means "star," or Hadassah, meaning myrtle, was raised by her older cousin Mordecai in Susa, the capital of Persia. She, along with fifteen hundred other virgins, gets taken into the harem of King Ahasuerus (Xerxes), the world's most powerful king, after he divorced Vashti, his queen, for arrogantly disobeying a direct order. A search began for a new queen and a country-wide beauty pageant ensued. Each young woman prepared to meet the king for a full twelve months of beauty treatments. Can you even *imagine*? The twelve months would ensure none of the women were pregnant when they went into the king. "Six months with oil of myrrh and six months with perfumes and preparations for beautifying women" (Esther 2:12).

One whole year of spa treatments? Where do I sign up?

When each woman's turn came to spend the night with the king, she took whatever beautiful garments, costly oils, and jewels she desired with the goal of attracting the king and hoping he would find her appealing. Basically, she had one night to impress the king and win his heart. Because after that night, unless he asked for her specifically by name, she would never spend another night with the king and she would live the rest of her life in obscurity among the other women of the harem. She would be relegated to the life of a concubine, not a wife, and certainly not a queen.

When Esther's turn came, unlike the other women, she went directly to Hegai, the king's eunuch and the custodian of the women, to ask him what *he* thought she should take into the king's presence. She knew Hegai knew the king well, and she knew Hegai would know just what the king liked. Hegai would know what style of dress the king favored, what jewelry and colors he liked, what subjects he found interesting, what perfume he preferred, and so on. She would take his advice, and by doing so, she gave herself a huge advantage over all the other women in the harem. Esther had the edge!

I believe one simple thing set Esther apart from the other women of the harem—she sought the king, not the luxurious lifestyle. She wanted *him* more than she wanted the gifts he could give her. Perhaps the other women sought the position or the beautiful clothing and pampered lifestyle of the harem. Esther, on the other hand, was laser focused on pleasing the king and not herself. Esther had already obtained the favor of Hegai, and as a result, she received extra-special beauty preparations, seven additional maids, and the "best place in the house of the women" (Esther 2:9). She was already being treated like royalty, a little foreshadowing of what was to come.

By intentionally taking time to find out what pleased the king,

Esther earned favor, honor, and a position of influence. Because she sought to know what pleased *him*, he fell in love with *her* and made her queen. God raised her from obscurity to prominence, position, and fame in one well-researched and well-thought-out night with the king.

As the story continues, it turned out God's favor in Esther's life had a specific purpose—an important task Esther would be offered and something much bigger than she could *ever* imagine. Something much more than position, beautiful clothes, and an opulent lifestyle. Along with position comes influence, and God was getting ready to triple-dog dare Esther in a huge way. He began preparing her for the biggest bungee jump of her life! She would soon find out if she would choose to be chosen.

It's true the name of God is never once mentioned in the book of Esther, which has caused concern to some. But God's influence and the Holy Spirit's fingerprints are all over her story. Deep humility and spiritual maturity mark Esther's life in her submission to her cousin Mordecai. The timing of her fast and the way she revealed her Jewish heritage to the king shows the wisdom, restraint, and guidance of the Holy Spirit. Her call for a three-day fast suggests she sought divine help. Mordecai's assurance that deliverance would rise from somewhere speaks to the guiding of Providence. God's name may not be mentioned, but His work is evident—He *will* protect and deliver His treasured possession, His people.

After Esther becomes queen, a nasty, ruthless villain named Haman, a descendant of Agag and an Amalekite, enters our drama. Haman, like the enemy of our souls, is prideful, vindictive, and bent on the destruction of the Jewish people.

Haman convinces the king to sign into law a decree to kill and annihilate all the Jews in his kingdom on a day set twelve months in the future. The king isn't yet aware Esther is Jewish because Mordecai forbade her to reveal her heritage to anyone. Mordecai finds out about the decree, and of course, he's horrified. Esther heard the deeply troubling news as well. Mordecai sent her a copy of the decree so she could read it for herself and go in to the king to plead for her people. But Esther is no spiritual example at this point in the story. She exhibited more concern for her own skin until Mordecai gave her something bigger than herself to think about. Maybe God wanted to convey He will use anyone in any position if they are willing to be used. But Esther felt extreme unease since she knew well that anyone, even the queen, "who goes into the inner court to the king, who has not been called, he has but one law: put all to death, except the one to whom the king holds out the golden scepter, that he may live. Yet I myself have not been called to go in to the king these thirty days" (Esther 4:11).

She hadn't seen the king, her husband, in a month—and I understand her reluctance because she knew the law required death to any uninvited guest in the king's court. Why hadn't he summoned her in a month? Maybe someone else had caught his eye, maybe her favor was waning. So Esther refused Mordecai initially with the reminder she would likely be killed if she went in to the king's presence without being called. Would Esther willingly risk her position? Her position could quite easily have become her prison. Truly, who can blame her? She knew she faced likely, if not certain, death. But she didn't yet realize God had positioned her for *precisely* this reason. Listen to what Mordecai said next, and see if you can hear the God Dare in his well-known words:

> *"Do not think in your heart that you will escape in the king's palace any more than all the other Jews. For if you remain completely silent at this time, relief and deliverance will arise for the Jews from another place, but you and your father's house will perish.* **Yet who knows whether you have come to the kingdom for such a time as this?"** (Esther 4:13–14, emphasis added)

Did you hear God's Dare? Esther most definitely did. It's almost as if God said, "I didn't bring you this far. . .for you to only go this far."

Digging deep and mustering all her courage, Esther took God's life-threatening dare. She risked losing everything but didn't stagger at the fear of death. Wagering her life, she instructed Mordecai to gather all the Jews in Shushan to fast for her for three days. She and her maids fasted as well, consuming no food and no drink. And she told Mordecai, "And so I will go to the king, which is against the law; and if I perish, I perish!" (Esther 4:16).

Counting the cost and growing up in that moment, Esther took God's triple-dog dare, grabbed hold of the bungee cord, and with fear and trepidation, I'm sure, Esther jumped. She knew she would likely crash. Yet with courage and great faith she jumped anyway, hoping against hope her God would catch her before she shattered on the rocks below.

Here's how the story ends: Esther and all the Jews in Shushan fasted for three days. At the end of the fast, she risked everything and stepped into the inner court of the king. The moment the king saw her, "she found favor in his sight, and the king held out to Esther the golden scepter that was in his hand" (Esther 5:2).

Phew! With enormous courage Esther risked her life, and in the end God afforded her the divine opportunity to reveal her heritage to the king and how it was wicked Haman behind the vile plot to annihilate her people. Haman ended up hung on the wooden scaffold he had erected for Mordecai (because Mordecai had refused to bow down to him), and the Jews were given the opportunity to fight back on the appointed day in the future. They did fight back and won the day, and since that time, for centuries, the Jews have celebrated the feast of Purim during the month of Adar (March–April).

Now in the twelfth month, that is, the month of Adar, on the thirteenth day, the time came for the king's command and his decree to be executed. **On the day that the enemies of the Jews had hoped to overpower them, the opposite occurred, in that the Jews themselves overpowered those who hated them.** (Esther 9:1, emphasis added)

See what I mean about rewriting history? I just love how our obedience can turn things around! There are so many wonderful lessons in the book of Esther, but what stands out to me is Esther's pure heart, her courage, and her willingness to take a huge leap of faith, a gigantic God Dare, risking her life for something she never planned on or asked for. Something far bigger than herself.

She's an ordinary girl blessed with extraordinary beauty, wisdom, and tact, and unbeknownst to her, God positioned her *exactly* where she would be most effective. She stepped up when courage was required and stepped into history and her divine destiny. She understood her position gave her influence, and it was incumbent on her to use her position for the greater good. And she did. She took the triple-dog dare. She went way out of her comfort zone and risked *everything* because that's what a spiritual bungee jump is all about. God chose a unique destiny for Esther—and He's chosen one for you and for me. You too have a sphere of influence, probably bigger than you realize. What opportunity is God dropping in your path? You never know what God is positioning you to do in the future!

Scriptures to Think About

- *For we are His workmanship, created in Christ Jesus for good works, which God prepared beforehand that we should walk in them.* (Ephesians 2:10)
- *For I say, through the grace given to me, to everyone who is among you, not to think of himself more highly than he ought to think, but to think soberly, as God has dealt to each one a measure of faith.* (Romans 12:3)

- *"And He has made from one blood every nation of men to dwell on all the face of the earth, and has determined their preappointed times and the boundaries of their dwellings."* (Acts 17:26)
- *"For whoever desires to save his life will lose it, but whoever loses his life for My sake will find it."* (Matthew 16:25)
- *Without faith it is impossible to please God.* (Hebrews 11:6 NIV)
- *"Do not think in your heart that you will escape in the king's palace any more than all the other Jews. For if you remain completely silent at this time, relief and deliverance will arise for the Jews from another place, but you and your father's house will perish. Yet who knows whether you have come to the kingdom for such a time as this?"* (Esther 4:13–14)

God Dare Secrets

- God is still looking for heroes and world-changers. Spiritual bungee jumpers who faithfully believe He will catch them. He triple-dog dares them, and they take the leap of faith, and their lives and our world are never the same.
- Faith only becomes real when it's tested.
- Faith is the doorway into trust.
- Sometimes God allows a mountain in your life to prove it CAN be moved. What's your mountain?
- Favor isn't always fair.
- Some God Dares change history.
- There's no testimony unless there's a test.
- God loves to use nobodies and change them into some-bodies for His kingdom.
- Some God Dares are life and death.
- God didn't bring you this far to only take you this far.

Discussion Questions

- In what ways has your faith ever been deeply tested?

- Has God positioned you in a place of influence? Are you willing to use your influence to change the world?

- What would it look like to lay down your life for God?

- If God has blessed you with position, beauty, or favor, how are you willing to let Him use it for *His* purposes?

- If God asks you to lay something down, will you? Will you trust Him to bring it back to life?

Chapter 6

THE WIDOW

As soon as I got in my van, I burst into tears and sobbed, "Lord, what is going on?" I drove home the first night after a deep and moving time of worship and fellowship with a sweet women's group at my friend's house. "What do they have that *I* don't have? I can't understand how these women love You. They speak of an intimacy with You, and I don't even know what they're *talking* about. *What is going on, Lord?*" As stinging tears streaked my cheeks, I drove home completely devastated.

Here's what was going on—God was using women I knew and loved and respected to birth a deep hunger in me for more of God, drawing me out into the deep ocean of a level of love and worship I'd never experienced before.

I'd been a Christian for a few years at this point. We'd moved from our quaint home in New Jersey and relocated to the Orlando area when our daughter turned seven. We came to love the dappled sun that sparkled through the palms and adored splashing in our backyard pool. We grilled out a lot and shared many meals together with new friends on our warm and inviting patio. As we began to put down roots in a new church, I started singing again and Mike played trumpet on the worship team. . .and God gave us forever friends. We shared meals and parties, hurts and losses with these folks. But I had no idea of the depths of love and worship God would expose me to.

I connected with a group of women much further ahead in their relationship with God than me. After the first evening I spent with them just worshipping, crying, laughing, and talking about Jesus, I remember how utterly dejected I felt. It wasn't anything anyone did, not at all; it's just that they had something I didn't have. I knew a lot *about* God by this time, but I didn't have what I would call an intimate relationship with Him.

I knew God, and I loved Him for what He could give me. But I had it all wrong, and being around these ordinary women who loved Him in an extraordinary way, simply for *who He is*, and who knew Him intimately. . .well, it made me feel intimidated, desperate, and hungry for more at the same time. Thank God for friends who make us hunger for more of Him!

Many of these sweet ladies were involved with the worship and arts team during those years, and I had opportunities to spend lots of time and even travel with them to conferences and such. Their examples of loving and pursuing God stuck with me and birthed in me a desire to really know Him, not just know *about* Him. I'm still on the journey, but I am eternally grateful to this group of women for mentoring me early on and for birthing a hunger in me that's still going strong. I honor these women today because they were in many ways the Naomis to my Ruth, the ones whose love for God shone bright no matter the circumstances in their lives.

I just adore the book of Ruth. She epitomizes the Old Testament picture of fidelity, humility, constancy, and hope. Her very name means "friendship," and she radiates loyalty. Let's take a look at her subtle but life-transforming God Dare.

The book of Ruth is a poetic short story set during the dark and blood-soaked time of the Judges, an era of spiritual confusion and deep apostasy. It's a pastoral idyll that takes place in the countryside during the turbulent Bronze Age years, before kings began to reign in Israel. This precious narrative presents life in its real and messy reality, with its tragedies and triumphs, its sorrows suffered and hopes realized. All the elements of a good story—romance, comedy, tragedy, danger, providence—are all packed into the four short chapters of a deeply moving and beautifully tender love story. A treatise on God's sovereignty and illustrating His sustaining mercy, the book of Ruth begins with loss and death but ends with fruit and life.

It's one of the few biblical narratives told from a woman's perspective with women as the main characters. Ideal womanhood is exemplified in Ruth, well before Boaz enters as the ultimate hero, the one foreshadowing the Lord in his kindness to Ruth and in his role as kinsman-redeemer.

Naomi is Ruth's sad, depressed mother-in-law, and though her name means "pleasant, delightful, and lovely," her life has taken a bitter turn. Living in a foreign land and bereft of husband, sons, or grandchildren, she has but one option left after the loss of her loved ones—and it's to return to her home in Bethlehem, the "house of bread." Like all Hebrews, Naomi is familiar with the one true God, likely weaned on the stories of the patriarchs and their desert wanderings and miracles. Even though her concept of God's great love for her is flawed, nevertheless her devotion to Him shines bright. I can easily picture Naomi drawing water, weaving, scrubbing, cooking, and worshipping even when life has ripped away her husband and sons. She knew her God, and though her understanding of His ways wasn't complete, her love was true.

Lovely Ruth observes Naomi's devotion as clear as day. She has seen Naomi's strength in the midst of death, loss, and devastation and her determination to "walk and not faint" (Isaiah 40:31) birthed a hunger in Ruth so deep that any hold her pagan gods may have had on her was shattered.

Even in Naomi's brokenness and the wreckage of her shattered dreams, a spark lingered, a belief in a God who knew her. And she knew Him and loved Him. In spite of losing everything, Naomi possessed the one true thing. In the deep sorrow of Naomi's sad life,

Ruth saw in Naomi the sustaining power of knowing God, and she too had to know Him. She couldn't *not* follow.

The divine God of the universe shone truth into Ruth's heart and poured quenching water into her thirsty soul. Ruth had lost her husband, Naomi's son, so she and Naomi shared a title neither would have chosen: *widow*. And like a drowning man bear-hugging a life raft, *Ruth clings*. She clung to Naomi because she saw something shining through her own pain and widowhood. *All Ruth thought she needed was replaced by what she had to have.* And she would leave behind her family, her homeland, and her gods to possess it. Ruth and Naomi illustrate a beautiful, moving, ancient sisterhood.

For some of us the God Dare is as clear and obvious as it was for Moses. I mean, you can't really ignore a bush burning hot with fire but not consumed. Sometimes the God Dare is for a specific reason, like Esther's dare to save her nation. And sometimes it's subtler and harder to decipher, that is, unless you're tuned into God's divine frequency.

Ruth's God Dare is much like that. It didn't shout from the mountaintops or appear in a dream. She didn't see an angel or hear God's voice. She simply heard and saw something raw and pure in the ruins of another's life, and regardless of the cost, her determination to follow drove her forward. So she followed and she clung. . .and her life was utterly changed.

Here's how it all happens. The book of Ruth begins during a time of crushing famine in Israel. Bread is scarce, so Naomi (*pleasant, delightful,* and *lovely*) and her husband, Elimelech, (*my God is king*) and two sons, Mahlon and Chilion (whose names mean "*weak* and *sickly*," and "*failing* and *pining away*"), leave Bethlehem and move to Moab, a land across the Dead Sea, and no friend of Israel. The Moabites were descendants of Lot after he fled Sodom and hid in a cave with his two virgin daughters. A rather unsavory episode followed where a drunk Lot impregnated both of his daughters and each had a son. One he named Moab, the other Ben-Ammi.

So although the Moabites were related to the Israelites, deep animosity existed between the two cultures, and the Moabites were not considered part of the nation of Israel because they worshipped false gods like Chemosh who required depraved and bloody child sacrifice as part of worship. The Israelites considered Moabites foreigners, and though marriage to a Moabite wasn't forbidden, a child born wouldn't be allowed into the congregation of Israel until the tenth generation. So after a decade of sojourning in Moab, Naomi's husband died and her two sons married Moabite women, Ruth and Orpah, and then, after another decade, her two sons died as well, childless.

Naomi, now widowed, childless, grieving, and destitute after twenty years away from her homeland, plans to return to Bethlehem when she learned the unrelenting famine had ended there at last. She urged her daughters-in-law to stay in Moab, find new husbands, and have children. Both initially refused. Naomi did her best to convince them of the futility of accompanying her, as she was unable to produce any more sons for them. And even if she could, would they want to wait the years until they were grown? With great sorrow she says, " 'No, my daughters, for it is exceedingly bitter to me for your sake that the hand of the LORD has gone out against me.' Then they lifted up their voices and wept" (Ruth 1:13–14 ESV).

Sounds like they all had a good, ugly cry. It's interesting to note that although Naomi felt deep devotion for God, she held a flawed perception of Him. She mistakenly believed His hand had "gone out against" her. What she didn't know, and what we so often cannot see, is His work behind the scenes. She had no idea of the incredible events and prosperous future destined for her. Naomi was being set up for blessing, but she didn't realize it yet. However, even with her misunderstanding of God's character, Naomi presses on.

Now comes one of my favorite lines in all of scripture as well as the dividing line between those who *say* and those who *do*: "Then they lifted up their voices and wept again. And Orpah kissed her mother-in-law, but Ruth clung to her" (Ruth 1:14 ESV).

Ruth *clung*. I imagine her giving Naomi an enormous bear hug and not letting go! Orpah looks back to her people and her gods, and though she'd promised to go with Naomi, perhaps her future and comfort meant more to her than she realized. We don't know for sure, but all I can think is Orpah counted the cost and found it wanting. She preferred the status quo and took the path of least resistance, choosing *her* gods over the one true God. We never hear from Orpah again.

Ruth, on the other hand, *clung*. She held on to Naomi for dear life and wouldn't let go. In Hebrew the word is *dabaq*, meaning to "hold fast." Why did one kiss and one cling? I'm convinced Ruth *saw* rather than heard the God Dare. Ruth witnessed Naomi's life day in and day out, in the drudgery and loss, amid heartache and sorrow, and sensed something at work far bigger than she understood. What she glimpsed ignited a burning hunger for more of God deep in her spirit.

Naomi's life illustrated her raw devotion to the one true God and sparked a hunger in Ruth impossible to satisfy by returning to the cruel and demanding gods of the Moabites. Ruth apprehended the God Dare in Naomi's everyday life, and in her imperfect faith she made the decision to trade the known—the life she'd likely experience had she returned to Moab—for something bigger, something she couldn't quite put her finger on, but it satisfied and drew her more deeply than the gods she used to worship. She sought "a better country" (Hebrews 11:16 NIV). Ruth didn't know it yet, but she was moving from famine to fruitfulness in a huge way!

I love the way F. B. Meyer in his *Devotional Commentary* describes Naomi:

> May not something also be said for the mother? It was because of her that Ruth was led to her supreme self-giving. She had never seen a suffering soul bear itself so heroically. She felt that in the Hebrew faith there was something which Chemosh had never imparted to her people; she craved for herself some of the holy radiance that lingered on the worn face of Naomi. More people watch our bearing than we think. Let us attract them to Jesus![3]

So beautiful, humble Ruth refused to settle for the world's *less* and chose the "holy radiance" manifested as Naomi's *more*—more truth, more life, more future, even if in that moment their future together looked bleak. Ruth clung and followed, taking the subtle God Dare. And because of her bold choice, Ruth is eventually dropped in the middle of the genealogy of Christ; Ruth, a Gentile and despised Moabite, became the great-grandmother of the greatest king in the Bible, King David.

Naomi continued urging Ruth to turn back. Ruth then spoke some of the most precious and beautiful words in all of scripture, words of a love so devoted, so deeply heartfelt they're often used in wedding ceremonies. I like to read them in the King James Version because of the gorgeous language: "And Ruth said, Intreat me not to leave thee, or to return from following after thee: for whither thou goest, I will go; and where thou lodgest, I will lodge: thy people shall be my people, and thy God my God: Where thou diest, will I die, and there will I be buried: the LORD do so to me, and more also, if ought but death part thee and me" (Ruth 1:16–17 KJV).

---

[3] F. B. Meyer, *Devotional Commentary* (Wheaton, IL: Tyndale House Publishers, 1989), 113.

"And thy God my God." Ruth answers the God Dare right there. She has decided to follow the one true God. Five simple words propel Ruth into a future she couldn't begin to imagine. So Naomi stopped trying to convince her to stay behind, and together they began the long journey back to the "house of bread." Here's where things start to get interesting.

As they arrive in Bethlehem, the whole city gets excited. Commentators believe Naomi likely came from an aristocratic family, which explains the commotion upon their arrival.

> *Now the two of them went until they came to Bethlehem. And it happened, when they had come to Bethlehem, that all the city was excited because of them; and the women said, "Is this Naomi?" But she said to them, "Do not call me Naomi; call me Mara, for the Almighty has dealt very bitterly with me. I went out full, and the LORD has brought me home again empty. Why do you call me Naomi, since the LORD has testified against me, and the Almighty has afflicted me?" So Naomi returned, and Ruth the Moabitess her daughter-in-law with her, who returned from the country of Moab. Now they came to Bethlehem at the beginning of barley harvest.*
> (Ruth 1:19–22)

Why would the city be stirred by these two poor, weary, hungry, and haggard women returning home? They had nothing concrete to offer—no money, no home, no position. But Ruth and Naomi were in exactly the right place. They were warmly received as they arrived at the perfect time—"at the beginning of barley harvest." Barley is harvested in late April, early in spring, as barley is the first grain to ripen. Barley is the "firstfruits" of the harvest. The beginning of the barley harvest after the long, cold winter brought great joy and worship from the people.

So the barley harvest began, and Ruth goes to glean in the fields. Gleaning is a directive in Israelite law, which required farmers to leave part of the harvest in the corners of the field for the poor, the aliens, and the widows to gather up. Ruth wins the Bible trifecta, because she is all three—poor, foreign, and a widow! By "chance" she ends up in the field of Boaz.

Providence, don't you think? She just *happened* to end up there. Riiiight. God knew well of her loyalty and devotion to Naomi, and He directed her perfectly into the path of Boaz, a relative of Naomi, whom the Bible describes as "a man of great wealth" (Ruth 2:1).

As divine providence would have it, Boaz, considerably older than Ruth, is a relative of Naomi's deceased husband. . .and Ruth ends up in *his* field. Boaz noticed how hard she worked gleaning in the hot sun, and he wanted to find out who she was. He directed her to stay in his field with his young women and commanded his men not to touch her—as in those times, gleaning could be dangerous. When Ruth questioned why she found such favor in his eyes, he responded that he had heard all she had done for her mother-in-law by leaving her own family and land to humbly serve Naomi. He blessed Ruth, rather prophetically I believe, that the Lord would repay and fully reward her and that she would come under His wings.

And Boaz answered and said to her, "It has been fully reported to me, all that you have done for your mother-in-law since the death of your husband, and how you have left your father and your mother and the land of your birth, and have come to a people whom you did not know before. The LORD repay your work, and a full reward be given you by the LORD God of Israel, under whose wings you have come for refuge."
(Ruth 2:11–12)

Boaz doesn't know it yet, but it's *his* wings Ruth is about to come under for refuge, and *he* is about to become her reward. Like Abraham, Ruth left behind everything—her father, mother, and native land to go to a country she didn't know. She left behind everything familiar. And like Abraham, God had bigger plans for her life than she could begin to imagine. He really does do more than we could ever ask or think, doesn't He?

People are watching us! They are watching what we do and how we live. They see by our actions if we're living righteously by living out our faith and if we're living with humility and bearing up under difficult circumstances. Boaz had heard all about Ruth and her diligent service to Naomi, and it intrigued him. Little did he know at the time, *he* was the one God would choose to bring her into her destiny.

So the story continues, and Boaz directed his men to allow her to glean among the sheaves, letting ripe bunches of grain fall purposely for her. At the end of a long, tiring day of gleaning Ruth brought home such an abundance of fresh grain that Naomi casually asked her whose field she worked in that day. Ruth responded with the name Boaz. Naomi praised the Lord and let Ruth know he was one of their close relatives. So Ruth faithfully continued to glean until the end of the barley and wheat harvests, about two more months. Day in and day out, she walked to the sun-scorched fields, bent down and picked up the barley and wheat left for her and the other gleaners. And she continued to honor and serve her mother-in-law and exhibit godly character and humility to everyone around her.

Savvy Naomi formed a plan for Ruth to persuade Boaz to marry her. She gave her instructions that today seem odd—she instructed Ruth to bathe, anoint herself with fragrant oils, put on her best clothes, and go down to the threshing floor where the men were winnowing barley. She would stay hidden and wait until Boaz fell asleep then go lie down and uncover his feet.

And Ruth does exactly what Naomi tells her to do.

> *So she went down to the threshing floor and did according to*
> *all that her mother-in-law instructed her. And after Boaz*
> *had eaten and drunk, and his heart was cheerful, he went*
> *to lie down at the end of the heap of grain; and she came*
> *softly, uncovered his feet, and lay down. Now it happened*
> *at midnight that the man was startled, and turned himself;*
> *and there, a woman was lying at his feet. And he said, "Who*
> *are you?" So she answered, "I am Ruth, your maidservant.*
> *Take your maidservant under your wing, for you are a close*
> *relative."* (Ruth 3:6–9)

At midnight the chilly air awakened Boaz, and discovering a woman at his bare feet, he asked who she was. Ruth answered and essentially asked Boaz for his protection because he was a close relative of Naomi.

It's difficult to understand these verses in the context of our modern times, as they deal with rather abstruse customs. But it's clear Ruth makes herself known to Boaz by asking for protection and assistance, and it's likely her actions implied marriage. Boaz is delighted a younger woman has taken interest in him, and he promises to do all that she asks. He mentions there is a relative even closer than he to Naomi but tells Ruth he will speak to him that day and see if he will fulfill his family obligation. Before she returned to Naomi, Boaz loaded her shawl with a large amount of ripe barley. Because Ruth is willing to obey Naomi's instructions and humble herself, she set herself up to receive great provision, position, and blessing. God is getting ready to turn everything around for Ruth and Naomi.

Ruth returned home to Naomi laden with an abundance

of grain—about seventy to eighty pounds' worth (it was not uncommon for laborers to carry that much in those days)—and she relayed the events of the night. Naomi assured her Boaz wouldn't rest until he took care of the issue. Boaz went, as promised, to the other close relative to find out if he would buy the land of Naomi's dead husband and make Ruth his wife. The relative refused when he found out he would be required to marry Ruth, so Boaz was free to make Ruth his wife.

They *do* marry, and Ruth conceived and bore a son! Naomi, who began this story bitter and empty is now filled with joy and restoration. Ruth, who had nothing to gain and everything to lose, gained everything! Ruth left behind the life she knew to follow and *to cling* to what mattered. She clung to truth and devotion and found a future and a hope, a husband and a son. Her son became the father of Jesse, the father of David, and she became one of only four women whose names are listed in the genealogy of Jesus Christ.

Sometimes the God Dare will draw you because of the example shown in another's life, a life exuding the fragrance of Christ. And in that case what can you do but follow? May all of our lives cause the Ruths who are watching *us* to follow and to cling!

Scriptures to Think About

- *These all died in faith, not having received the promises, but having seen them afar off, and were persuaded of them, and embraced them, and confessed that they were strangers and pilgrims on the earth. For they that say such things declare plainly that they seek a country. And truly, if they had been mindful of that country from whence they came out, they might have had opportunity to have returned. But now they desire a better country, that is, an heavenly: wherefore God is not ashamed to be called their God: for he hath prepared for them a city.* (Hebrews 11:13–16 KJV)

- *"For I know the plans I have for you," declares the* L*ORD*, *"plans to prosper you and not to harm you, plans to give you hope and a future."* (Jeremiah 29:11 NIV)
- *But they that wait upon the* L*ORD* *shall renew their strength; they shall mount up with wings as eagles; they shall run, and not be weary; and they shall walk, and not faint.* (Isaiah 40:31 KJV)
- *Now to Him who is able to do exceedingly abundantly above all that we ask or think, according to the power that works in us, to Him be glory in the church by Christ Jesus to all generations, forever and ever. Amen.* (Ephesians 3:20–21)
- *And Ruth said, Intreat me not to leave thee, or to return from following after thee: for whither thou goest, I will go; and where thou lodgest, I will lodge: thy people shall be my people, and thy God my God: Where thou diest, will I die, and there will I be buried: the* L*ORD* *do so to me, and more also, if ought but death part thee and me.* (Ruth 1:16–17 KJV)

God Dare Secrets

- No matter what culture we come from, the God Dare is available to everyone.
- Sometimes your life is another's God Dare.
- People are watching our lives more than we realize.
- The generations desperately need one another.

Discussion Questions

- How have you seen God move in someone's life in such a pure way you were determined to follow?

- In what ways has another believer sparked a deep hunger in you to know God better?

- Have you ever sparked that hunger in someone else? How do you know?

- Are you willing to choose God's *more* and relinquish the world's *less*? What might that look like?

- Who is watching you as you live out your faith? Would they want to follow what they see in your life? How do you know?

- Are you willing to let your life become another's God Dare?

Chapter 7

THE PRINCE OF EGYPT

I figured out early in life that math and science were not my strong suit. I'm a little embarrassed to admit I struggled to pass algebra with a D...and believe me when I tell you I was happy just to pass! In spite of my dismal performance in math, from childhood on, I've adored English, poetry, and creative writing.

One of my proudest moments arrived in ninth grade when I got accepted into the AP creative writing class, an advanced high school English class back in the late '60s. My best memory happened when my teacher actually asked for copies of my haikus. I was simply bursting with pride! I loved to write, and I loved to read, but I never dreamed in a million years I'd actually *become* a writer.

What I failed to realize during those years and for many years of journaling afterward is this simple fact: God laid a deep foundation for a time to come much later in life when I'd long forgotten about my love of writing. He knew it was a gift I would need and delight in later in life, so He laid the foundation in my youth. He then let the gift lie fallow while I pursued other gifts and talents and life dreams, including theater, music, marriage, and motherhood.

But to everything there truly is a season, and like Moses, in the fullness of time and when it served His purpose, the time came for me to dust off my love of writing, take my own personal God Dare, and write my first book.

Moses is the one the Bible calls the humblest man who ever lived, and he can teach us much about the God Dare. Let's go back several millennia and take a look at Moses, born a Hebrew but adopted by Pharaoh's daughter and raised as a royal son in the Egyptian court who chucked it all to be with his people. The Hebrews had no use for Moses' help at first, so after secretly killing an Egyptian (or so he thought until one of the Hebrew men called him out), Moses ran for his life! I think Moses knew leadership lay deep in his DNA, but God's timing wasn't in his equation. He *would* lead, eventually, but Moses was nowhere near *ready* to lead. In fact, he totally blew it by acting in his own strength. Let's take a look at how it all unfolds.

From Sweetheart to Sweat Hog

Moses, the tiny baby pulled out of the muddy Nile by Pharaoh's daughter, goes out from the royal court one day forty years later to see how burdened his brethren, the Hebrews, are by Pharaoh's oppressive commands. He witnesses an Egyptian beating a Hebrew man, and when he thinks no one is watching, he kills the Egyptian and hides his body in the sand. The next day he happens upon two Hebrew men fighting and steps in to stop the fight. They know all about what he did the day before, so they ask who made him judge over them. Then they ask if he's going to kill them like he did the Egyptian. Busted!!

Moses just *knew* he was the one to deliver his people, so in his own strength and with righteous indignation, he killed an Egyptian. His people were oppressed and in bondage, and Moses convinced himself he was the one to lift their burdens. So he killed an Egyptian he found fighting with a Hebrew. Pharaoh finds out, and terrified he's been discovered, Moses races into the desert to hide. God allows him to be driven into utter discouragement for forty years. *Forty years.* Somehow Moses sensed he was the one to deliver his people, but he had to undergo severe training and discipline before God could use him. At the end of forty years in the desert, all he can say to God is, "Who am I that I should go?"

Our efforts for God without His anointing are doomed to failure.

Moses ends up in the land of Midian (a name meaning "strife" or "place of judgment"), where the Bible says *he sits down* at a well. Seven sisters, the daughters of Jethro the priest of Midian, come to the well to water their flocks, and Moses helps them fetch their water. This scripture in the book of Acts pretty much sums it up: "For he supposed that his brethren would have understood that God would deliver them by his hand, but they did not understand" (Acts 7:25).

You think? Moses went from sweetheart to sweat hog in quick order.

From Failure to Forerunner

His own people don't want him to rule over them, and, scared and intimidated, Moses runs away and then *he sits down*. Let's jump ahead forty years. So there's Moses in the back of a hot, lonely desert leading stinky sheep for decades. Solitary days and cold nights and lots of "sitting down." I'm sure he wondered why on earth he was pulled out of the Nile as a baby, raised in Pharaoh's court, trained to rule and to judge, and now the only thing he's judging is sheep. And sheep bite. I have an inkling Moses looked back on his life feeling like an utter failure. But oftentimes failures become forerunners and sweat hogs become sweethearts. "And Moses was learned in all the wisdom of the Egyptians, and was mighty in words and deeds" (Acts 7:22).

After forty years do you think it's possible Moses imagined he'd totally missed his purpose? Do you think he might have doubted and questioned God? Do you think he believed his actions in the past disqualified his future? Might he have wondered why on earth he'd been saved as a baby, raised in Pharaoh's court, and trained to lead, yet his life couldn't be further from that reality? Think about it: four decades have passed at this point.

Did God allow total discouragement to overtake Moses' life? He rightly discerned God's call, but the missing link for Moses, and for so many of us, involved *decades* of God's careful training. How often our training ground lies in the desert! It's not about us; but *it's about us learning who God is.* And some of us learn that lesson best in the arid and barren desert. I'm convinced the solitude of the desert is one of God's favorite training grounds. Moses *would* become "a prince and a judge" (Exodus 2:14) over the people. But just not in his way or his timing. Forty years of humility training would precede his destiny to lead.

In the Turning Comes the Calling

After forty years of shepherding on the backside of the desert (and having all the pride worked out of him), one day Moses saw a remarkable sight—a burning bush ablaze in the distance. Remember Moses is eighty years old by now, and at his advanced age he is probably tired. So who would have blamed him if he ignored a bush on fire? Or perhaps he thought he was seeing a desert mirage. But Moses did not ignore the bush. He made a crucial, life-changing, history-altering decision and said, " 'I will now turn aside and see this great sight, why the bush does not burn.' **So when the LORD saw that he turned aside to look, God called to him**" (Exodus 3:3–4, emphasis added).

In the turning came the calling. I love the idea of God watching Moses like a hawk to see what he would do. No one had heard from God for centuries, but all of a sudden He calls to Moses. And in that moment of decision, at the intersection of curiosity and hope, when the Lord saw that he turned aside to look, *God dared him.* My modern-day paraphrase goes something like this:

> "Moses, you've been leading sheep for forty years on
> the backside of this desert. I've been watching you and

training you, and now I've chosen you to lead my chosen people for another forty years, out of bondage and oppression and into a land flowing with milk and honey because I really *have* chosen you to be a prince and a judge over my people, just like you thought forty years ago. You were absolutely right, but I had to work some things into you and *out of you* before I could use you to change the world. It won't be an easy road because I'll harden Pharaoh's heart. But after I strike Egypt with all my wonders he'll eventually let you go. And you won't go empty-handed; in fact, you'll plunder the Egyptians on your way out of town. So, what do you say, Moses?"

Elizabeth Barrett Browning says this: "Earth is crammed with heaven, and every common bush afire with God, but only he who sees takes off his shoes."[4]

I wonder, for those of us who've been rejected for something we were *certain* God was calling us to, did the seeds of it actually coming to pass perhaps lie in the rejection? Moses had to live with his rejection and uncertainty *for forty years*, which is a very long time to be unclear about your purpose, believing you've missed it. But in those intervening years, Moses—the man who God said was "mighty in words and deeds"—now described himself thus: "Then Moses said to the LORD, 'O my Lord, I am not eloquent, neither before nor since You have spoken to Your servant; but I am slow of speech and slow of tongue'" (Exodus 4:10).

Tongue-tied Moses experienced deep humility training in the intervening years. In his time of waiting, all pride had been entirely worked out of him, so much so that God declared him the humblest man who ever lived. This great leader, raised as royalty, now being called by God Himself to lead and deliver his people,

---

[4] "Aurora Leigh" (Chapman and Hall, 1857).

finally finds out he was right all along. God wanted to do it *His* way and in *His* time.

We know how the story ends. Moses took the God Dare, with exceeding reluctance and great trepidation (and with his brother Aaron's help), and he substantially changed history. God laid it all out to Moses—how stubborn and hardhearted Pharaoh would prove to be and how difficult the task would be to accomplish—and *everything* God told Moses came to pass.

God is watching you and me too. He drops opportunities into our paths and ideas into our lives and new connections and possibilities. . .and waits to see if we, like Moses, will "turn aside and see this great sight." Will you take a hard look at the opportunity or idea offered you and see if it's part of God's purpose for your life? And if it is, are you willing to pay the price to accomplish His purpose? Are you willing to take the God Dare? Are you willing to be used to change the world, even if it takes forty years of humility training in order to come to pass? There will be a moment when the door opens and lets the future in.

What's the *great sight* you're deciding whether or not to take a look at? God is watching! Moses had all the necessary training he needed to lead the people of Israel into the promised land. Forty years in the royal court and another forty in the desert worked into Moses all he needed to lead a great nation and bring the Israelites out of idolatrous Egypt and into their destiny as God's chosen people.

You've been trained too, especially those of you reading this who may be older and think life has passed you by. I believe Moses most certainly felt that way. I just bet he scratched his head in wonder when he thought about his past and the years of his life he perhaps imagined were wasted. What Moses didn't know is this: the desert is one of God's favorite training grounds. Moses may well have imagined he'd missed his purpose and calling, convinced somewhere along the line he just didn't get it right. But he couldn't have been more wrong!

As I've said before, God's economy is never wasteful and He never squanders the life training He gives us. He will use *everything* you've gone through when you trust Him to lead. God will call out the big dream He placed in your heart decades earlier and give it wings. Both Abraham and Moses prove you are never too old for God to use you—and both of these remarkable biblical heroes changed the world.

Whether you are over the age of fifty or sixty (like I am) or eighty, it doesn't matter to God. In fact, I'm convinced He especially likes to use us when we're older. It proves all the more clearly we can't change the world in our own strength but only in His. You are never too old to be used by God, and if that's your excuse for not taking the God Dare, please reread the stories of Abraham and Moses and ask God to change your heart!

I want to make one other point about Moses. The old staff he used to herd his sheep for forty years became the same staff God turned into a serpent, the same staff he used to strike the Nile, turning it to blood, the same staff he used to strike the Red Sea to part it so the Israelites could pass safely through, and it's the same staff he used to cause the plagues to strike the Egyptians. If we've been faithful with it, God will use whatever we have in our hands to change the world.

Check out Exodus 33:11. "So the LORD spoke to Moses face to face, as a man speaks to his friend." How amazing! Moses reluctantly takes God at His word, leads the Israelites out of Egypt, gets angry more than once, and doesn't do everything perfectly, yet God speaks to him face-to-face as a man speaks to his friend. Can you even imagine? That makes taking the God Dare worth *everything*.

Scriptures to Think About

- *"This Moses whom they rejected, saying, 'Who made you a ruler and a judge?' is the one God sent to be a ruler and a deliverer by the hand of the Angel who appeared to him in the bush. He brought them out, after he had shown wonders and signs in the land of Egypt, and in the Red Sea, and in the wilderness forty years."* (Acts 7:35–36)

- *"I will now turn aside and see this great sight, why the bush does not burn." So when the LORD saw that he turned aside to look, God called to him.* (Exodus 3:3–4)

- *By faith Moses, when he was born, was hidden for three months by his parents, because they saw that the child was beautiful, and they were not afraid of the king's edict. By faith Moses, when he was grown up, refused to be called the son of Pharaoh's daughter, choosing rather to be mistreated with the people of God than to enjoy the fleeting pleasures of sin. He considered the reproach of Christ greater wealth than the treasures of Egypt, for he was looking to the reward. By faith he left Egypt, not being afraid of the anger of the king, for he endured as seeing him who is invisible. By faith he kept the Passover and sprinkled the blood, so that the Destroyer of the firstborn might not touch them.* (Hebrews 11:23–28 ESV)

- *So the LORD spoke to Moses face to face, as a man speaks to his friend.* (Exodus 33:11)

- *"And it shall come to pass in the last days, says God, that I will pour out of My Spirit on all flesh; your sons and your daughters shall prophesy, your young men shall see visions, your old men shall dream dreams."* (Acts 2:17)

- *Then Jesus, being filled with the Holy Spirit, returned from the Jordan and was led by the Spirit into the wilderness.* (Luke 4:1)

- *Then Jesus returned in the power of the Spirit to Galilee, and the news of Him went out through all the surrounding region.* (Luke 4:14)

God Dare Secrets

- Age doesn't excuse you from hearing and taking the God Dare.
- Oftentimes we have to "turn aside and look" before God calls us.
- In the turning comes the calling.
- Some of us will go from sweetheart to sweat hog and back again.
- One of God's favorite training grounds is the desert.
- Jesus went into the desert in fullness. . .and He came out in power.
- God will use whatever you have in your hand to accomplish His purposes if you've been faithful.
- Each of us has an assignment to change the world.
- Like the bush on fire, we can burn with God's holy passion and not be consumed.

Discussion Questions

- Do you think God's forgotten you or you're too old for the God Dare? Why?

- Do you think perhaps you've missed God because of failures in the past? How?

- Do you believe your past disqualifies you from being used by God? Why?

- Will you pay whatever price to accomplish God's purpose? What do you think the price might be?

- What "sight" do you need to turn aside and take another look at?

- Does God have you in a desert season right now? What does that look like?

Chapter 8

THE SLAVE

The day before, Franny had backed straight into a lawyer's car. It was completely her fault and she felt mortified it happened at all. Truth be told, it happened right in the lawyer's driveway immediately after the lawyer told her, "Be careful you don't back into my car!"

Driving home after the fender bender and crying and feeling like a complete failure, she began to sing what she was hearing, as if God downloaded a chorus right into her spirit. He began to speak to her heart, reminding her she wasn't perfect and He loved her anyway. He had created her the way she was, and her only task was to trust Him. So, as God comforted her heart, she began singing this song about dents in her fender and rips in her jeans. Franny and I used to joke during those years about how God would continually humble us. We seriously thought about making up T-shirts that said, "Just call 1-800-HUMBLE-ME." (I might make them anyway since He continues to find new and clever ways to humble us!)

The next day our sweet and contrite Franny called us into her bedroom telling us she wanted to play a new song for us. We were always eager to hear her newest creation, so we sat on the end of her bed as she picked up her guitar and played this catchy, amazing song. The song stunned us in its simplicity and beauty, and as soon as she finished I said, "Franny, I don't know what to tell you, but that's a hit song right there. I don't know how I know, *I just know.*"

In fact, the Lord was sharing a little glimpse of the future with me years before our daughter moved to Nashville, signed a record deal, or had a song on the radio. And three years after singing her catchy song to us in her bedroom, "Free to Be Me" became the first single by a female artist to hit number one on Christian radio in eight years—and it stayed at number one for ten weeks and received a GRAMMY nomination!

I didn't share what I was feeling with anyone but my husband and daughter at the time, because some dreams are better fought for in prayer, especially the crazy big ones. But I had a certainty right then and there and a knowing deep in my spirit God had something big planned for our little girl.

The Price of the Anointing

Have you ever had a "Joseph dream," one you're hesitant to share because people will be convinced you're absolutely crazy? Or the kind of dream so scary and so big it's best kept under wraps because folks will think you're an arrogant egomaniac if you share it? Yeah, *that* kind of dream. Those dreams are less common because if they're truly from God you may well have a Joseph road ahead of you.

Dreamers Stir Up Haters

Joseph, the patriarch Abraham's great-grandson, the next-to-youngest of Jacob's twelve sons and a mere teenager, experienced dreams of a leadership role he couldn't begin to comprehend. His youthful exuberance and lack of maturity caused him to share his dreams prematurely, and he couldn't help but rub it right in his older brothers' faces. So God took him on a long and winding road in order to mature and equip him to handle the place he'd been shown in his dreams.

Here's a truth: *There's a price for dreams, and big dreams are costly.* When God shows you the mountaintop, frequently the way up will first take you down into the valley of humility. Joseph goes from the pit to the palace and eventually becomes prime minister of Egypt. But first he will face a long and deeply painful journey. Like Moses, Joseph goes from sweetheart to sweat hog and eventually back to sweetheart again.

He must have known he was Jacob's favorite, Rachel's eldest son, with his vibrant, flashy multicolored coat. His brothers most certainly did. I'm sure he used the favor of his father and his privileged position to his advantage whenever he could, hugely annoying his brothers. In fact, they couldn't stand the sight of him! To add insult to injury, Joseph shared one too many lofty dreams of his brothers bowing down to *him*. And believe me when I tell you, his brothers were *done*. Joseph even shared a dream where he saw the sun, moon, and eleven stars bowing down to him. This caused his brothers to despise him big-time. Even his adoring father began to question Joseph's dreams.

One day Joseph's brothers were off tending their sheep in Shechem, so their father, Jacob, sent young Joseph to check up on them. But as they saw him approaching in the distance in his colorful coat, Joseph's envious brothers devised a cruel and wicked plan. They couldn't stand the sight of Joseph, so they determined to once and for all rid themselves of him. Be certain of this: there are those who can't handle your dreams and they will do all they can to kill them in order to abolish your future and elevate their own.

Joseph's brothers were jealous enough to heartlessly murder Joseph, that is, until Reuben, the firstborn of Jacob's sons, intervened. Reuben convinced Joseph's envy-filled brothers to compromise and sell poor Joseph, who was all of seventeen years old, pampered and favored, into slavery. Ruthlessly torn from the only world he knew, stripped of his gaudy coat and thrown into a pit, Joseph is thrust into a life he never dreamed of or asked for. All because as an immature teenager, he couldn't keep his mouth shut or his dreams to himself and because jealousy reared its ugly, family-shattering head. Joseph had vision, and there are those who will persecute *anyone* with vision.

What his brothers didn't realize is this: God used their betrayal to catapult Joseph directly into his destiny. They thought they were ending Joseph's dreams. In their minds I'm sure they believed they would never see him again. But no matter how broken your dreams may seem, God has a plan, and He is working faithfully behind the scenes to bring them to pass.

God had some big life lessons in store for our Joseph. In truth, God really *did* call him to lead. In the future, Joseph's family *really would* bow down to him, but he had no idea how or why. God had a master plan in place for Joseph, and he would be utterly transformed as God breathed life into that plan. But first Joseph needed to learn this important lesson: in God's economy *submission always precedes promotion*.

God Sees Us According to Our Destiny, Not Our History

After his brothers sell Joseph to Midianite traders for twenty pieces of silver, Joseph is sold at the slave market to Potiphar, an officer in the court of the pharaoh of Egypt and captain of the guard. A remarkable scripture just casually sits there and it's quite easy to miss: "The LORD was with Joseph, and he was a successful man" (Genesis 39:2).

Seriously? A successful man? Based on what? The fact that his brothers hated him enough to murder him? Psalm 105 says this about Joseph: "He sent a man before them—Joseph—who was sold as a slave. They hurt his feet with fetters, he was laid in irons. Until the time that his word came to pass, the word of the LORD tested him" (Psalm 105:17–19).

With feet in fetters and body in irons, I don't know if I'd feel particularly successful. But God sees us according to our destiny, not our history. The fact is Joseph *was* successful in the middle of desperate circumstances. He was successful because God was with Joseph. God ordered each and every one of Joseph's steps, in spite of the fact his brothers rejected and abandoned him. So after first being sold as a slave to Midianite traders, the traders now sold him to Potiphar in the bustling Egyptian slave market. Favor and position come to us in the oddest places, don't they? What Joseph had been given by Almighty God was determined, planned, set in stone, and could not be taken away. But first Joseph would indeed be deeply tested by "the word of the Lord."

God began preparing Joseph to enter thirteen years of humility training, but he had no idea. I'm convinced that the higher God plans to take you, the lower you'll be required to humble yourself in order to learn the same crucial lesson Esther had to learn: success and position are not about you. Joseph needed training to humble his heart so he could fully walk into his calling to change the world and save his family and the future nation of Israel from destruction. The tiny seed of the nation of Israel, the promise given to Abraham, in fact *the destiny of an entire people group* rested in Joseph's hands. But he didn't have a clue.

So teenaged Joseph found himself sold to Potiphar, the captain of Pharaoh's guard, and he went to live and serve in Potiphar's house. Joseph worked diligently, and Potiphar quickly noticed that everything Joseph did prospered. As a result, Potiphar elevated Joseph and made him overseer of his entire household, giving him authority over everything Potiphar owned. Everything, that is, except his wife.

"The Lord was with Joseph and he was a successful man." So because God was *with* Joseph, Potiphar's house, his land, his crops, his cattle, his *everything*, experienced blessing. Maybe when the Lord is with us and we are *successful*, everything we come in contact with is blessed too.

And his master saw that the LORD was with him and that the LORD made all he did to prosper in his hand. So Joseph found favor in his sight, and served him. Then he made him overseer of his house, and all that he had he put under his authority. So it was, from the time that he had made him overseer of his house and all that he had, that the LORD blessed the Egyptian's house for Joseph's sake; and the blessing of the LORD was on all that he had in the house and in the field. Thus he left all that he had in Joseph's hand, and he did not know what he had except for the bread which he ate. (Genesis 39:3–6)

Whatever Joseph touched prospered. God was with him, and because God had already called him successful, he experienced success wherever God placed him. Joseph's leadership and organizational skills were evident to all, and as a result Potiphar put him in charge of a large and bustling Egyptian estate. Potiphar acknowledged that the Lord was with Joseph. There was just something about this cocky kid devoted to his God and who worked hard at everything he was tasked to do day in and day out!

Everything went well for Joseph for a while, that is, until Potiphar's sexy wife joined the party and noticed the young and talented Joseph. He was—how do people say it today?—hot! "Now Joseph was handsome in form and appearance. And it came to pass after these things that his master's wife cast longing eyes on Joseph, and she said, 'Lie with me'" (Genesis 39:6–7).

She wanted access to her own boy-toy so she flat out propositioned Joseph to sleep with her (and people think the Bible is boring!).

But Joseph maintained his high standards and a strong moral conscience. Note: this is more than four hundred years *before* the Ten Commandments have even been given. There was no commandment against adultery in writing or in practice, yet Joseph maintains his fear of the Lord, clearly valuing holiness above all. I'm convinced he'd heard many stories about the Lord from his father Jacob, his grandfather Isaac, and his great-grandfather Abraham. He must have been aware of his lineage and the important role it played in recent history. He had an important part to play too, something special he would be tasked to do, and because of his dreams, I believe he knew it. After relentless temptation from Potiphar's wife, Joseph made a remarkable statement: "There is no one greater in this house than I, nor has he kept back anything from me but you, because you are his wife. How then can I do this great wickedness, and sin against God?" (Genesis 39:9).

Joseph recognized sleeping with another man's wife as a sin against God, not simply a sin against Potiphar. However, day after day, week in and week out, she hounded Joseph relentlessly, begging him to sleep with her. One day when they were alone in the house together, this Old Testament cougar attacked. She caught him by his coat, but Joseph pulled away, leaving his coat in her hands, running out of the house naked. That makes two times Joseph had a coat torn from him.

To save her reputation, Potiphar's wife lied and accused Joseph of attempted rape. Potiphar believed his wife and swiftly condemned Joseph to prison. In doing what Joseph knew to be the right and honorable thing, he still found himself repaid unjustly. However, even in prison God stuck with Joseph, and he quickly gained favor with the keeper of the prison. He put the administration of the entire prison under Joseph's authority. Joseph's path had been predetermined by God, and He allowed Joseph to bear these difficult tests. And Joseph repeatedly stepped up to the challenge with God's favor securely resting on all he did.

The Lord was with Joseph in prison, the lowest place he could sink to, and yet, he couldn't help but prosper. Remarkably, once again Joseph found himself in a leadership position, albeit at the lowest low of his life. I have a theory and I believe Joseph's story bears it out: God loves opposites and often uses them to *prove* us. In fact, our ups will often be determined in the depths of our downs.

For example, if God is going to fill us, He will empty us. If He is going to clothe us, He will strip us. Before He takes us up the mountain, He takes us down into the valley. And if He is planning to make us wealthy, He will first bankrupt us. God will allow the exact opposite condition in our lives to see how we deal with it. We can only rise up to the degree we are prepared to go low. And the lower we are willing to go, the higher He can exalt us. "And whoever exalts himself will be humbled, and he who humbles himself will be exalted" (Matthew 23:12).

I love how Oswald Chambers says it. It describes Joseph perfectly: "We have no right to judge where we should be put, or to have preconceived notions as to what God is fitting us for. God engineers everything, wherever He puts us our one great aim is to pour out a whole hearted devotion to him in that particular work, 'whatsoever thy hand findeth to do, do it with thy might.'"[5]

From the Pit to the Palace

No matter his circumstances, as the years clicked by Joseph kept earnestly working and endeavored to do his best. His work and leadership were clear to all despite his lowly position. Joseph is the poster boy for making lemons out of lemonade. In fact, Joseph proved the destiny of the diligent. "The hand of the diligent will rule, but the lazy man will be put to forced labor" (Proverbs 12:24).

Eventually Joseph was given the opportunity to use his other skill set: dream interpretation. Pharaoh had put his butler and baker into prison, and Joseph dutifully served them both. One night both the butler and baker had vivid dreams they didn't understand. They took them to Joseph for interpretation. Joseph replied: "Do

---

[5] Oswald Chambers, *My Utmost for His Highest*, April 23.

not interpretations belong to God? Tell them to me, please" (Genesis 40:8).

So they do, and Joseph correctly interpreted both. The butler was reinstated in his position, but the baker was doomed to execution, just as Joseph predicted. Joseph asked only one thing of the butler when he was reinstated into Pharaoh's court. He requested the butler mention him to Pharaoh and help him get released from prison. Joseph knew he'd been falsely imprisoned but had no recourse, no voice, and no way to be set free.

Of course, the butler totally forgot about Joseph. In fact, the Bible says another *two full years* went by. Do you think Joseph could even *hear* his God Dare or any possibility of his dreams coming to fruition any longer? Two more years of humility training for Joseph, and I imagine he began to think this may well be as good as it will ever get. But two more years of training are necessary in order for Joseph to utterly and completely die to self. . .and that's when Joseph becomes ripe for promotion. Sometimes God seems strangely silent and absolutely nothing seems to be happening or changing. But silence isn't always a sign of God's displeasure. Often, times of silence are times of discipline to ready you for your future.

One fateful night two years later, Pharaoh had two terrifying dreams. None of his magicians or wise men could interpret these dreams, but suddenly the forgetful butler remembered Joseph and how he correctly interpreted his and the baker's dreams two years earlier. So Pharaoh sent for Joseph and asked him to interpret the dreams. I adore Joseph's answer, which proves positively his humility training is complete and he's ready for promotion: "Joseph answered Pharaoh, 'It is not in me; God will give Pharaoh a favorable answer'" (Genesis 41:16 ESV).

Joseph completely deflected any credit and ability on his own and tells Pharaoh it has nothing to do with him but is completely God's domain. His humility training is finished!

Joseph tells Pharaoh flat out he can do nothing of his own strength or gifting and only God can give the interpretation. He is the perfect Old Testament example of *death to self* and knowing that apart from God he is nothing. At this season of his life, thirty years old and having spent half his years as a slave or in prison, wondering, hoping—some days I imagine doubting there was any kind of future for him—everything shifts. The season suddenly changes, a fresh wind blows, and after correctly interpreting Pharaoh's dreams, Joseph is lifted out of prison and given the second-highest position in the land. Fifteen years of training in leadership and humility, and Joseph finds himself positioned to save the world.

Even pagan Pharaoh recognizes the Spirit of God in Joseph. He says, "Can we find such a one as this, a man in whom is the Spirit of God?" (Genesis 41:38).

Here's how it all turns out for our Joe. Deeply impressed by this young Hebrew prisoner and realizing Joseph possesses divine wisdom and discernment, Pharaoh appoints him second in command over all of Egypt. He gives Joseph his signet ring, garments of fine linen (it sounds like he gets a new coat!), a gold chain, and a wife. His authority can only be eclipsed by Pharaoh's. Talk about going from the pit to the palace!!

And in one day our dreamer's dreams begin to come true. Joseph receives position, promotion, honor, authority, favor, and family. His wisdom and discernment, diligence, and humility have set him apart, and though it took years of training, life begins to look up for Joseph. But Joseph's story doesn't end there, not by a long shot.

The Bible informs us there is a severe famine, so every country in the world comes to Egypt to buy grain from Joseph. I'm fascinated by the fact that God knows He is going to deliver the nation of Israel out of Egypt some four hundred years later and that they are going to come out with "great possessions" (Genesis 15:14). In fact, they will "plunder the Egyptians." God sent Joseph not only to save the nation of Egypt from famine, but he was sent centuries ahead to save the Israelites. Joseph led the seed of the nation of Israel *into* Egypt and Moses would lead millions *out!*

Time passes and the seven years of plenty Pharaoh dreamed about are complete, and the seven years of famine begin. By now, Joseph has two young sons named Ephraim and Manasseh and he's become governor over the land. Anyone who wants to buy grain *must* come to Joseph.

"The famine was over all the face of the earth, and Joseph opened all the storehouses and sold to the Egyptians. And the famine became severe in the land of Egypt. So all countries came to Joseph in Egypt to buy grain, because the famine was severe in all lands" (Genesis 41:56–57).

There was severe famine in Israel too, so Joseph's father Jacob, when he learns there is grain in Egypt, sends ten of his sons— Joseph's half brothers—down to Egypt to buy food. He keeps Benjamin, his youngest son and Joseph's little brother, behind. And in the very next verse as Joseph's brothers stand before him, the far-fetched dream God gave Joseph years before comes true: "And Joseph's brothers came and bowed down before him with their faces to the earth" (Genesis 42:6).

Fifteen years have gone by and his brothers didn't recognize Joseph. . .but *he* recognizes *them.* Dressed in fine Egyptian clothing and speaking Egyptian, Joseph appeared before them as an Egyptian ruler. The brothers had *no idea* they'd just fulfilled prophecy in a significant way. Joseph questioned them, refusing to let them leave and return to Israel. He put them in prison for three days (maybe to give them a little taste of what he dealt with during his years as a slave and a prisoner) until they agreed to travel back to their father—being allowed to return to Egypt *only* if they agree to bring their youngest brother, Benjamin, back with them.

The brothers return to Israel, and after some time as the famine rages on, they once again begin to run out of food. Reluctantly, their father Jacob sends them back to Egypt with Benjamin, his youngest son. Benjamin was Joseph's only full brother, the other son of Jacob and his beloved favorite wife Rachel, who died shortly after giving birth to him. After eating a meal with his brothers, Joseph tricks them by filling their sacks with grain and instructs his steward to put his silver cup in Benjamin's sack as he sends them on their way. The brothers head home but before long the steward catches up to them and says, "Why have you repaid good with evil? Isn't this the cup my master drinks from and also uses for divination? This is a wicked thing you have done" (Genesis 44:4–5 NIV).

So the steward searches their sacks and finds the planted cup in Benjamin's sack. Cue the music! They all return to Joseph, and suffice it to say, they have no way to explain what happened. Joseph announces Benjamin will have to stay in Egypt and become his slave, but Judah realizes that if Benjamin, as the only surviving son of Jacob's cherished wife Rachel, stays behind, it would likely kill his father, so he humbly offers to stay in Benjamin's place.

Joseph can't keep up the charade any longer, and with many tears and heartfelt emotion he finally makes himself known to his brothers. Of course they are *terrified*! I'm certain this is the *last* thing his brothers ever expected—Joseph is alive and ruling over the entire nation of Egypt! I imagine they might be thinking, *How in the world did this happen?* But Joseph in his humility, discernment, and wisdom now speaks a great truth to his brothers. He shares how it wasn't *them* who sent him to Egypt, but God. "But God sent me ahead of you to preserve for you a remnant on earth and to save your lives by a great deliverance. So then, it was not you who sent me here, but God" (Genesis 45:7–8 NIV).

Joseph's dream as a teenage boy served a huge purpose, one

bigger than he could have *ever* imagined. God put a plan in place to save the entire Hebrew race, and Joseph was the one He'd chosen to carry it out. God knew Egypt would be the place of multiplication for His chosen people, and in His sovereignty, God sent Joseph ahead to make a way for his family where there was no way. Remember this scripture from the beginning of the chapter: "Until the time that his word came to pass, the word of the LORD tested him." God *will* test us, especially if He gives us a Joseph dream.

Joseph never got the chance to return home to Israel, but I imagine during all those years in Egypt he longed for home and the familiar land where he'd grown up. Maybe that's why he made his brethren promise to bring his bones home with them when they left Egypt. It took four hundred years, but Moses finally brought Joseph home. Do you know where *your* home truly is?

Sometimes the God Dare is in the crazy huge dream you don't yet understand, but even if you don't understand it, God can bring it to pass one way or another. Hopefully, if a dream like Joseph's comes to you, God won't allow you to be sold into slavery or put in prison. Truth is, not all dreams are meant to be shared. If you do receive a Joseph dream, ask the Lord for discernment before you tell the world!

Scriptures to Think About

- *The plans of the diligent lead surely to plenty, but those of everyone who is hasty, surely to poverty.* (Proverbs 21:5)
- *"But God sent me ahead of you to preserve for you a remnant on earth and to save your lives by a great deliverance. So then, it was not you who sent me here, but God."* (Genesis 45:7–8 NIV)
- *The LORD was with Joseph, and he was a successful man.* (Genesis 39:2)
- *"And whoever exalts himself will be humbled, and he who humbles himself will be exalted."* (Matthew 23:12)

- *And Joseph's brothers came and bowed down before him with their faces to the earth.* (Genesis 42:6)

God Dare Secrets

- We will only rise to the degree we're willing to go low.
- God sees us according to our destiny, not our history.
- Even if your dreams have been shattered, know God is at work on your behalf, behind the scenes.
- There are those who can't handle your dreams, and they will try to kill them to abolish your future.
- Having a destiny doesn't mean you'll never suffer. It almost guarantees you'll suffer.
- There's a price for the anointing, and big dreams can be costly.
- There are those who will persecute anyone with vision.
- God will allow the opposite circumstance in our lives to test us. How we respond will determine our destiny.
- Submission always precedes promotion.
- Just call 1-800-HUMBLE-ME.
- Sometimes taking the honorable road is repaid with injustice.
- It takes courage to answer the calling on our lives so others can receive their inheritance.
- Times of silence are often times of discipline, not times of displeasure.

Discussion Questions

- What big dream has God given you that you might be scared to share with others?

- How will you maintain high standards and a strong conscience in the middle of temptations?

- Have you ever had a big dream come true? What did it look like and feel like?

- Has God's Word ever tested you? If so, how?

- If God is calling you to position and authority, how has He taught you the crucial lesson that it's not about you?

- Are you willing to humble yourself and take the lower place to let God exalt you in His timing? How do you know?

- Are you in a season of God's silence right now? What might He be trying to teach you?

Chapter 9

THE PROSTITUTE

A prostitute in the lineage of Christ? How very fitting the way God proves in His Word that *anyone* can be washed by His blood and be utterly transformed, cleansed, and made fit for His purposes. And how like Jesus to love and honor women so well! It's interesting we think of Rahab as a prostitute, yet twice in the New Testament she's held up as a woman of faith. Check out Hebrews 11:31 and James 2:25. Once again, thank God He sees us according to our *destiny*, not our *history*.

We all face impossible situations in our lives with circumstances requiring God to come through in a *big* way. Challenges like infertility, major health issues, divorce, addictions, depression, miscarriage, etc. Seasons and situations we have no control over, and our only hope is in God coming through for us.

Impossible is what God does. It's what He's known for. He's an expert at impossible situations. He's famous for raising the dead, opening blind eyes, giving children to folks way past childbearing age (remember Abraham and Sarah, or Elizabeth and Zacharias?). God owns the impossible, but He's given us an ability I find *incredible.*

We Possess the Possible

We have more than enough talent and brains to do much more than we are currently doing. Why don't we do more? I know a few reasons (ahem, *excuses*) because I've used them for years. But recently, God has pointed them out to me and won't let me slither off the hook any longer. He reminds me how He presents the possible to me every single day. He tells me over and over, "Possess your possible." When I do, I see miracles.

When I don't, typically my number-one excuse is laziness. Number two? Fear. Fear of what people might think, fear of rejection, fear I won't do a good job, fear that I really don't deserve good things.

People say if you see it, you can believe it, but lately that little expression is getting turned on its ear. What I'm hearing is, "If you believe it, you will see it." After all, we can't see faith. It's "the substance of things hoped for, the evidence of things not seen" (Hebrews 11:1). If you don't have faith to believe it, you will never, ever see it. Paul, in Romans 4:17, straight-up tells us to call "those things which do not exist as though they did."

What comes next? We can call things *things* that are not till the cows come home, but without any action, without actually *doing* something, without getting out of our own way, getting up, and taking action, nothing will change.

It's time we grab hold of the possible. It's ours to possess—it's our promised land. The God Dare is found right at the intersection of the possible and the impossible. When God promised land to the Israelites, they had to go in and fight off the giants and the interlopers *first* in order to possess their land. It wasn't handed to them on a silver platter. God dared them with what was possible, and the rest He left up to them. We can leave the *im*-possible to God, He's the expert at it after all. But the possible? It's your turn to possess it because that's where the God Dare lives.

Is it hard? Yes. Will it take discipline? Absolutely. Will you have to give up some things? Probably. Will you be tempted to quit? For sure. Will it be scary? Of course. Will it be worth it to change your life and achieve your goals? I guarantee it.

My biggest enemies are laziness and fear, and let's throw in procrastination because that's *real life*. But I know folks from every walk of life who are possessing their possible and changing countless lives in the process. I've decided I no longer want to live in the land of *good enough*.

I don't believe God is stingy or wants to see any of us broke and depressed, sick and tired, unhappy and unfulfilled. He gives us all we need for life and health and happiness and what He does for one, He will do for all. He is no respecter of persons. But, you *will* have to do a couple things. You'll have to decide you are worth it, worth the work and worth the fight. You'll need to make some changes, get off the couch, pray like mad, and see just what is possible in your life. "All things are possible to him who believes" (Mark 9:23).

I'm always stunned by the size of Rahab's faith, her belief in the impossible, and her practical doing of what *was* possible in order to save herself and her entire family from destruction. Captured by God's fearsome reputation, Rahab risked her own life to save two Hebrew spies and ended up liberating her entire family. She threw in her lot with the spies, and risking everything, she possessed her possible for a God she'd only heard about, leaving all she knew for the One she *had to know*. Here's how it all came about.

Moses has died and Joshua, eighty years old, now leads the Israelites. God commands him to conquer the land, so he sends out two spies to see what they'll be facing, primarily checking out Jericho. Off go the two spies, and they arrive at the house of a harlot named Rahab. In those ancient days, harlots (prostitutes) were often well-respected priestesses of the Canaanite religion, so her profession may well have been considered reputable among her people.

Through divine providence, the two spies come to lodge at the one house in all of Jericho where they'll be welcomed rather than reported to the authorities. It's just like God to divinely arrange matters, and how like Him to use a pagan and a sinner to change history! Rahab dwelled in an inn where people would be coming and going all the time, so the foreign spies would be less apt to draw attention in the crowd. Yet of course someone noticed them and tells the king that Rahab has Israelite spies lodging at her house.

The king dispatches messengers to command Rahab to hand them over. But savvy Rahab had heard the stories of the Israelite conquests and she'd begun comprehending something wonderful about the God of the Israelites. Beginning to fear Him, Rahab did what any sensible woman would do. . .she hid the spies. She hid them because she'd decided to throw in her lot with Jehovah, the God she'd heard so much about, the one true God. What she'd heard was so awe-inspiring it caused her to "*tremble at His word*" (Isaiah 66:5), motivating her to risk her life to save the spies. Rahab believed life and death were in God's hands, and in spite of lacking any deep knowledge of God, what little she did know caused her to fear Him and act on His behalf. Can you hear the raw and deep awe in these words she spoke to the spies?

> "*For we have heard how the* LORD *dried up the water of the Red Sea for you when you came out of Egypt, and what you did to the two kings of the Amorites who were on the other side of the Jordan, Sihon and Og, whom you utterly destroyed. And as soon as we heard these things, our hearts melted; neither did there remain any more courage in anyone because of you,* **for the** LORD **your God, He is God in heaven above and on earth beneath.**" (Joshua 2:10–11, emphasis added)

Rahab's faith revved up to full force when she informed the spies she knew God would give the Israelites success. She shared with them how her people were absolutely terrified of the Israelites as they too heard how God dried up the Red Sea when the Israelites came out of Egypt. They'd heard the horrifying stories of all the peoples who'd been destroyed by them. She shares how she knew their God is the true God and asked the spies to swear to her that, because she helped them out, they would spare her and her family when they came to annihilate Jericho.

She declares, with faith and boldness, exactly who God is and exhibits complete trust in the God of the Exodus, about whom she has only heard, but never known. God's fierce reputation alone dared Rahab to trust Him, and trust Him she did, with determined boldness. She took the two spies up to her roof—hiding them under stalks of flax laid out to dry—brashly lying to the king's messengers and telling them yes, the men were there but they'd already left. Obviously, lying is rarely ever the right choice, but remember Rahab's faith is brand new at this point, and she's not yet been taught the Ten Commandments. So lying, in her world, seemed the right response to a dangerous situation.

After the king's men left, she let the spies down by a rope through her window, and crafty negotiator that she clearly was, made them first swear to her they would "show kindness to my father's house, and give me a true token, and spare my father, my mother, my brothers, my sisters, and all that they have, and deliver our lives from death" (Joshua 2:12–13).

Her faith may be immature at this point, but her heart for intercession is already well developed. She shows amazing compassion and loyalty to her family, demonstrating a growing faith already relying on God's promises.

Rather like Ruth, Rahab's faith is not impulsive. She'd heard the Exodus story and she trusted what she'd heard, making an educated decision to cast her lot with the Israelites and leave behind the life she'd known. How often does God call us, in fact, *dare us* to go? He *told* Abraham to go. He *forced* Joseph to go. Ruth *wanted* to go. Moses *had* to go. Rahab *determined* to go. When God captures your heart, the going will prove it.

The spies gave very strict instructions about whom they would and would not save—only those actually *in* Rahab's house at the time of conquest would be saved—anyone outside her walls would be destroyed along with the city. If a family member lingered outside her house when the destruction came, it would be too late. The spies told Rahab they would be blameless of the oath unless she placed a scarlet cord in her window so they could easily locate her home and leave it untouched. Her job then was to bring her father, mother, brothers, sisters, and her father's entire household into her house, so they'd be saved. She agreed to their terms, sent the spies away, bound the lustrous scarlet cord in her window and waited patiently for deliverance.

The beautiful "scarlet cord of redemption," the precious symbol of the blood of Christ, reaches through the centuries, across the testaments, from the blood smeared on the doorposts in Egypt protecting the firstborn from the angel of death in Exodus, to the blood running down the cross and wiping out our sin on Calvary in the Gospels. The symbolism is powerful! Rahab tied the scarlet cord in her window and protected her family from death. Thanks be to God His blood still covers and protects today!

God knew all about Rahab. In fact, in His wisdom, he orchestrated events to bring the spies directly to her house. He knew her sin and also her ignorance of His commandments. And because of her ignorance, God disregarded her sin of lying. He not only took her in but because of her faith, fearlessness, and intercession, gave her a position in the lineage of Christ. What a great lesson Rahab teaches us about not letting our past hinder our future. How great is His love toward all of us!

As time went by, I imagine the people were terrified out of their wits by the Israelite army silently and bizarrely marching around their city day after day. Yet I imagine Rahab, calm and certain of her salvation. F. B. Meyer says this in his *Devotional Commentary*:

It is not the amount of truth that we know which saves us, but the grasp with which we hold it. All that Rahab knew was very slight and partial, but she held onto it with all the tenacity of her soul, and it was accounted to her for righteousness (Rom. 4:5). She identified herself with Israel by the scarlet thread, gathered her kinsfolk under her roof, and waited in anticipation of deliverance (James 2:25).[6]

As the story continued, and the Israelites silently marched around Jericho seven times, Joshua commanded the two spies to go into Rahab's house and bring out all that she had, just as they'd negotiated. So they brought Rahab and her family out of Jericho and burned the city down, sparing only Rahab and her father's household and all she possessed because of her courage and stalwart faith when she hid the spies. The book of Hebrews says: "By faith the harlot Rahab did not perish with those who did not believe, when she had received the spies with peace" (11:31).

Rahab believed. She had faith. Her heart was at peace because her faith took over. God spared her life *because she received and didn't reveal*. Faith without works is dead, James says. Rahab's life, deeply treasured by God even in her grave sin, again proves He calls us according to our destiny, not our history. Rahab believed, acted with boldness, and earned herself a position in the lineage of Jesus Christ. "We walk by faith, not by sight" (2 Corinthians 5:7).

God is no respecter of persons. In fact, Rahab, the former prostitute, married Salmon, the son of a leader of the tribe of Judah. Rahab and Salmon became the parents of Boaz, the faithful and godly husband of Ruth, and Rahab now became Ruth's *other* mother-in-law. Nothing, *absolutely nothing* is impossible with God. No matter what your life looks like right now, God can transform any heart that's open to receive Him.

---

[6] F. B. Meyer, *Devotional Commentary* (Wheaton, IL: Tyndale House, 1989), 92.

Scriptures to Think About

- *You see that a person is justified by works and not by faith alone. And in the same way was not also Rahab the prostitute justified by works when she received the messengers and sent them out by another way? For as the body apart from the spirit is dead, so also faith apart from works is dead.* (James 2:24–26 esv)
- *By faith the walls of Jericho fell down after they were encircled for seven days. By faith the harlot Rahab did not perish with those who did not believe, when she had received the spies with peace.* (Hebrews 11:30–31)
- *Faith by itself, if it does not have works, is dead.* (James 2:17)

God Dare Secrets

- God calls us according to our destiny, not our history.
- We walk by faith, not by sight.
- When God calls us to go, the going proves our faith.
- Your past need never hinder your future.

Discussion Questions

- Has God dared you to go? Where has He called you? Will you go?

- Do you have faith to receive God's promises for your life? How do you know?

- What does it look like to be called according to your destiny, not your history?

- Are you willing to receive and not reveal?

Chapter 10

THE LEPER

Playwright Edward Albee wrote something in *The Zoo Story* years ago that's always stuck in my head: "Sometimes it's necessary to go a long distance out of the way in order to come back a short distance correctly."[7]

I never really understood this, because I heard it before I had lived it. Now? I understand *perfectly*. I learned the hard way that God's way is not my way. God is not a Ouija board, and He's not our own personal Magic 8-Ball or Santa-Jesus. His job isn't to satisfy our every desire and fulfill our every whim. And sometimes, He will take us a long distance out of the way in order to bring us back a short distance correctly. *He will take us out to bring us in.*

I've wanted lots of things in my life, good things mostly, but none so much as a big family. Children and babies under my feet, crayons, crumbs and chaos, toys and tantrums, Legos and sippy cups—messy and delightful like children always are. My very own Five Little Peppers all lined up on Easter morning, scrubbed shiny, with little man suits and lacy dresses, patent leather shoes and bow ties, all marching into church. My own fuzzy ducklings and me one proud mama. Big family blessings, fights and friendships, noisy meals around a big farmhouse table. My heart, my dream.

But God.

He had a different dream for my husband and me...not one we would have chosen, but when do we *ever* know what's best for us?

We didn't know when on Labor Day, over thirty years ago, I

---

[7] Edward Albee, *The Zoo Story* (New York Samuel French,1959).

almost died from an ectopic pregnancy, exploded fallopian tube and all.

We didn't know as the doctor explained my remaining tube was scarred and damaged beyond repair.

We didn't know as we wept over the finality of the infertility diagnosis.

We didn't know weeks later after they did the test shooting this dark dye into my nether regions to see if the surgery to open the remaining fallopian tube held.

We didn't know when the dye didn't shoot out of the tubes as it should have but pooled into a stagnant, evil Rorschach blot that mocked our pain.

The doctor was clear and clinical, dismissive even, in his diagnosis. "You won't be able to get pregnant again."

Have you ever actually *felt* your heart break? My future collapsed that day, my dreams imploded as hot tears gushed and hope crashed. "You can always adopt," he said. *Crash.* My ever-stalwart husband did the best he could. I remember asking the fertility doctor if my abortion years earlier had damaged my remaining fallopian tube. He unequivocally said, "Yes." I learned in that moment the terrifying truth of this verse: "Do not be deceived, God is not mocked; for whatever a man sows, that he will also reap" (Galatians 6:7).

We lived just outside Princeton, New Jersey, then, and our doctor practiced in Philadelphia. Whenever we had an appointment, we rewarded ourselves with one of those legendary and incomparable Philly cheesesteaks. That day was no different. By force of habit and love of food, even when our worst nightmare just came true, we drowned ourselves in hot chopped steak, gooey provolone cheese, caramelized onions, mushrooms, and soggy french fries and drove home shattered. Full but oh so empty.

God, in His wisdom and graciousness, had given us one amazing daughter two and a half years earlier. And now He was saying to us, *"Can that be enough?"* But it wasn't, not for a long, long time. This mama's heart was broken. Recovery was long, and three failed adoption attempts later, despairing. I learned, albeit slowly, how God always has future generations in view, and sometimes our disappointment and loss is about something far bigger than ourselves.

God knew in time that healing would eventually come and baby announcements and showers wouldn't continue to be pure torture. Going into Babies "R" Us wouldn't generate a rush to *get-the-heck-out-of-there-before-I-break-down* panic every time I had to buy a baby present. Self-pity, my favorite bad feeling, gnawed at my heart like a rabid dog with a bone, reminding me *Who* was really to blame. Eventually though, I did begin to heal.

As our daughter grew, she began to display astounding gifts and talents. God revealed to us how to help her dig deep and bring out those gifts, polish them up, and offer them to the world. He showed us her life would be a public one, her ministry large and far reaching, and she would need our full attention to help her get there. We embarked on our journey together, discovering the music business and learning all we could to help her launch her dreams.

After years of holding God hostage for not living up to my expectations, I eventually realized the value of what He had given me. One night at a women's conference during a time of deep worship, I heard Him whisper clear as a bell in the midst of my pity party, *"Am I enough?"*

And it broke me. He slipped out of the box I'd worked so hard to close Him in and did the unexpected. He gave us one child with a world-class gift, one with a purpose far bigger than I could ever have imagined, and He said, *"Can you take this on? Will you? Will you be satisfied with the road you're on, no matter where it leads?"* Then He took *my* heart hostage as He whispered, again, *"Am I enough?"*

God doesn't ask questions He doesn't have the answer for. So like Moses, I let Him answer. . . *"I AM."*

And He is. He is *everything*, and there's nothing I would trade for the life I've been privileged to live. God taught me during this painful season the most valuable lesson of all: to love Him for who He *is* and not for what He *gives*. In spite of my slow-to-learn heart and my ugly past, God gave us an incredible and loving child and now a wonderful son-in-law and four precious grandchildren. These darling little ones are my absolute heartbeats, letting me enjoy plenty of crayons, crumbs, and chaos. My four little peppers, precious little ducklings with a Mimi and Poppy devoted to the moon and back.

And that's how He answered my prayer for children. It was a *no*, but qualified. It took me a long time to get it through my aching heart and thick head, but eventually I did. And today I'm grateful, so very grateful, He took us a long distance out of the way in order to bring us back a short distance correctly.

When Small Things Make a Big Difference

God loves every person on earth, even those living in darkness and spiritual blindness. He proves over and over that whoever seeks Him *will* find Him. His grace and mercy are available to all if they will simply respond to His divine invitation, humble themselves, and trust Him. The story of Naaman proves even proud and stubborn hearts can take the God Dare and see their lives utterly transformed.

Naaman, a great commander in the army of the king of Syria, whom scripture calls a "mighty man of valor" (2 Kings 5:1), is also a leper. On one of his raids, he captures a young girl from Israel who now serves Naaman's wife. The servant girl can't help but mention the mightiness of her God and how she believes he could be healed of his leprosy if only he would go to the prophet Elisha who resides in Samaria. She's a young servant girl—we are never even told her name—who owns a big faith and truly knows who her God is, even though she herself is a slave, torn from her family and homeland. Naaman listens to this wise young girl and goes to the king of Syria, who decides to intercede on Naaman's behalf by writing a letter to the king of Israel.

How would you like to get a letter like this?

Now be advised, when this letter comes to you, that I have sent Naaman my servant to you, that you may heal him of his leprosy. (2 Kings 5:6)

Can you imagine what the king of Israel thought when he received that letter? He had no apparent relationship with God and clearly wasn't BFFs with Elisha. Naturally, the request in the letter angered him because he was convinced the king of Syria was trying to start a quarrel or a war by asking him to do the impossible. So the king of Israel did what they did back then when they got upset—he tore his clothes! Elisha hears about it and gets in on the action. "So it was, when Elisha the man of God heard that the king of Israel had torn his clothes, that he sent to the king, saying, 'Why have you torn your clothes? Please let him come to me, and he shall know that there is a prophet in Israel'" (2 Kings 5:8).

Elisha had bulletproof faith to say something like that. He had absolutely no doubt God would heal Naaman. Oh, if only more of us had the faith of Elisha today.

So off Naaman went to Elisha's house, riding ramrod straight in his chariot, expecting Elisha himself to come outside and do something spectacular to heal him of leprosy. He was an important guy after all! But instead Elisha, a prophet of the Most High, extended a quiet God Dare to Naaman in a most unique way. He gave Naaman this simple instruction by way of his messenger saying, "Go and wash in the Jordan seven times, and your flesh shall be restored to you, and you shall be clean" (2 Kings 5:10).

This offends Naaman BIG-TIME. He imagined Elisha would come out, call on his God, and wave his hands around making a big show of healing his leprosy. How often do we expect God to do a thing *our* way? We keep God in His little box, and when He dares us to let Him out, we say, "How dare You?"

When God asks us to do something that doesn't make sense to us, aren't we just like Naaman, saying, "No, God, that's impossible and silly. I'm totally *not* doing *that*." Naaman is about to learn a simple lesson: God opposes the proud and gives grace to the humble. And sometimes God will ask you to do something ridiculous before you see the miraculous.

So the Bible tells us haughty Naaman went away in a rage, all because Elisha didn't come out and make a big to-do of healing him.

Anger, pride, and offense can blind us to the truth of our God Dare if we let them. We expect our healing or deliverance to come in a certain way, and when it doesn't, we rage! Sometimes the simplest solutions are the hardest because they butt right up against our pride. But God in His gentleness convinces us one way or another, and sometimes He'll even use our friends or the people around us, which is what happened in this story.

> *And his servants came near and spoke to him, and said, "My father, if the prophet had told you to do something great, would you not have done it? How much more then, when he says to you, 'Wash, and be clean'?"* (2 Kings 5:13)

With great respect, gentleness, and tact his servants helped Naaman see Elisha's instruction from another perspective. Sometimes it's the small things that make a big difference. Naaman's healing will only begin when he humbles himself.

Naaman wisely decided to listen, set his pride aside, humble himself, and go down to the Jordan to dip seven times. Often God has to get us to the point where we will do *anything* to get our healing or deliverance, and sometimes He brings us to the end of ourselves before we'll listen. Thank goodness Naaman takes the God Dare, does the crazy dipping, and gets his healing. Scripture says his flesh was restored like the flesh of a little child. . . which sounds like baby-soft skin to me! He became a "new creature" by setting aside his prejudices, humbling himself, and putting his faith in the God of Elisha.

Naaman took the God Dare even when it looked like utter foolishness to him, and he got his life back. He went "a long distance out of the way in order to come back a short distance correctly." Overwhelmed by God's goodness, he asked Elisha for two mule-loads of earth so he could, commentators think, erect some sort of altar to Yahweh for worship in his own country. When he returned to his country he knew he would again have to live among unbelievers and be required to worship the false god of his master, so he asked Elisha: " 'When my master goes into the temple of Rimmon to worship there, and he leans on my hand, and I bow down in the temple of Rimmon—when I bow down in the temple of Rimmon, may the LORD please pardon your servant in this thing.' Then he said to him, 'Go in peace.' So he departed from him a short distance" (2 Kings 5:18–19).

Aren't we all lepers like Naaman, infected with the sin of pride and needing to be washed clean by the water of God's Word and by His precious blood? Without Christ, we're condemned to die, leprous and alone. But with Him, our sins are washed away. Naaman realized he had to go back to his world and his master's God, but after going through his trial, he knew without a doubt the one true God!

Naaman put aside his pride and took the God Dare. He proved

God to be all His reputation said He was. Imagine the stories he told when he returned to his country!

Scriptures to Think About

- *But He gives more grace. Therefore, He says: "God resists the proud, but gives grace to the humble."* (James 4:6)
- *Do not be deceived, God is not mocked; for whatever a man sows, that he will also reap.* (Galatians 6:7)
- *For the wages of sin is death, but the gift of God is eternal life in Christ Jesus our Lord.* (Romans 6:23)

God Dare Secrets

- God opposes the proud and gives grace to the humble. Don't let anger, pride, or offense cause you to miss your God Dare.
- Sometimes you'll have to go a long distance out of the way to come back a short distance correctly.
- Small things can make a big difference.
- If you *can* be offended, you *will* be offended.

Discussion Questions

- What do you find harder to deal with: anger, offense, or pride? Why do you think that is?

- Has God ever done something in a way you weren't expecting and didn't like?

- Do you recall a time when you would have done anything to receive healing? What were you required to do?

- What if God calls you to do something that seems ridiculous? Will you?

Chapter 11

THE FORERUNNER

When we've walked with God for any length of time, we find He entrusts us with a divine gift—the gift of suffering.

The Christian walk, this following in the footsteps of Jesus, this walking the narrow way, isn't for the faint of heart. It will take us to the limit of ourselves. We think we know Him until we go through the trial or the tragedy in life, and then, quick as can be, we accuse Him of abandoning us. We forget He told us, "In this world you will have trouble. But take heart! I have overcome the world" (John 16:33 NIV).

We want our very own "cocktail party Jesus" to grant us immunity from trouble; we certainly don't want to be *immersed* in it. In my own desperate struggle with infertility, I could not fathom how a loving Father could possibly treat me so poorly. If God gives us the desires of our hearts, why am I not getting mine? I would never treat *my* child that way, I'd rage.

> *"Or what man is there among you who, if his son asks for bread, will give him a stone? Or if he asks for a fish, will he give him a serpent? If you then, being evil, know how to give good gifts to your children, how much more will your Father who is in heaven give good things to those who ask Him!"*
> (Matthew 7:9–11)

God gives us bread and fish, yet we accuse Him of giving us snakes and stones, useless and thoughtless gifts. We wrongly judge when trials come. We forget He *entrusts* us with sorrow, with trials and difficult circumstances. He wants us to find the deeper joys of knowing Him, not just the surface happiness. But true joy *can* be found in the deep place of trust when absolutely everything is falling apart.

Can God trust you with silence? If He can, it means He knows you can handle a deeper revelation about His purpose. You thought He was giving you a stone but are finding instead it's the Bread of Life. You can handle the deeper place. His silence is a sign of His intimacy.

There's profound joy in knowing He will never leave us or forsake us. We only learn this truth when we've been left and forsaken by the ones we relied on. Only then does He become our all-in-all. Because there's a point to our suffering, it isn't random. We can comfort others "with the comfort with which we ourselves are comforted by God" (2 Corinthians 1:4).

We suffer as Christ suffered, for the consolation and salvation of others (verses 5–7).

God entrusts us with the gift of suffering for this purpose: to comfort others and show the depths of joy. God's desire for you is union with Himself. It takes time to develop, but in the time of suffering, when the clouds of your life are thick and you can't see the sun, when His voice goes silent and the pain is real, don't give in. Hold Him ever closer, and what you ultimately receive will be far more than you ever dreamed.

Sometimes the very dream you cling to, the dream giving your life purpose and joy, may not be God's dream for you. He may require you to lay down the worthy dream you hold so close. Because, and this seems crazy but it's true, God has something better than you could have imagined and all He asks is that you trust Him.

At times God may take away what we want, to test us and

to help us trust in Him more than anything else. One time Paul was suffering so much he thought he was going to die. But he knew God's purpose was good. God loved Paul with tough love. So Paul said, "Yes, we had the sentence of death in ourselves, that we should not trust in ourselves but in God who raises the dead" (2 Corinthians 1:9). God had a valuable purpose for Paul's pain. He was teaching Paul to trust *in Him* more than health and life.

Will you let Jesus pick? Does *He* get to decide what your life will look like?

Sometimes our God Dare won't look the way we thought it would when everything we thought we knew or believed about God gets challenged to the core. God will dare some of us to believe in the middle of tribulation where the only way out is death. Trust me when I tell you, the God Dare is *not* for the weak or timid.

When John the Baptist had been in prison for about a year, shortly before he died, he sent his disciples to Jesus to ask a burning question:

> *Now it came to pass, when Jesus finished commanding His twelve disciples, that He departed from there to teach and to preach in their cities. And when John had heard in prison about the works of Christ, he sent two of his disciples and said to Him, "Are You the Coming One, or do we look for another?" Jesus answered and said to them, "Go and tell John the things which you hear and see: The blind see and the lame walk; the lepers are cleansed and the deaf hear; the dead are raised up and the poor have the gospel preached to them. And blessed is he who is not offended because of Me." (Matthew 11:1–6)*

John is stuck in prison. And for what? For doing what God called him to do from the womb. He was chosen before his birth as the forerunner, the one sent to announce, the voice in the wilderness calling all to repentance. He'd been absolutely *certain* Jesus was the Christ, the Messiah, the Anointed One.

But now John languishes alone in a dark, dank prison for a year, held hostage by Herod Antipas, one of the most flagrant and scandalous sinners of those times. All because John publicly called out Herod's wicked sin of adultery with his brother's wife.

But if Jesus truly was the Christ, why couldn't He get John out of prison? Why did He allow John to be sent there in the first place? How did *any* of this even make sense? Doubt began to creep in, and John simply had to know the truth. Even a great man like John the Baptist was tempted to doubt, tempted to allow offense to creep in. No one is immune.

John was no wimp. Incredibly strong and devoted to God, he chose to live in the desert, dressed in scratchy camel hair, eating a diet of locusts and honey. He had no problem speaking truth to power and calling all to repent. I don't imagine there was anything soft about John the Baptist! But now he finds himself in a prison cell. In humility and desperation, he sent his disciples to ask Jesus if He was *really* the One or should he be looking for someone else? I can't really blame him. Don't we all question God when life stops making sense?

During this time in history, the Jews expected their Messiah to come and expel the tyrannical Gentile oppressors from their land and set up a political kingdom of righteousness and peace. Jesus was not exactly living up to their expectations. Little did they know He would die because of *them*. Jesus tried to make it clear, but really, until Pentecost and the coming of the Holy Spirit, most Jews simply didn't get it.

The profound words Jesus used to instruct John's disciples to share with him come primarily from Isaiah 61 and 35. However, Jesus leaves out one important detail: He never mentions this phrase: "To proclaim liberty to the captives, and the opening of the prison to those who are bound" (Isaiah 61:1). The one thing John most yearned to hear. In His wisdom, Jesus simply ignored this part, and perhaps John realized it was Jesus' subtle message letting him know he was *not* getting out of prison alive.

Haven't we all been there at some point? Circumstances change in our lives, difficulties descend, and all the tidy notions of who God is and how He works are thrown into chaos as life crashes around us. We can't see God *anywhere*, so we begin to doubt. We start adding up all the things we've done for Him wondering if any of this is real. We get mad and offended at God. "How could You, Lord? I thought You loved me? I thought we had a deal? I follow You and You bless me, right, Lord?" Religious entitlement swiftly rears its ugly head.

John the Baptist, the one who baptized Jesus, the one who actually saw the Holy Spirit descend on Jesus in bodily form as a dove, the one who heard God speak, "This is My beloved Son, in whom I am well pleased" (Matthew 3:17). This amazing prophet of God, the Elijah who was to come, had nothing to look forward to but a beheading. But hear Jesus' words about His beloved John:

> *"Assuredly, I say to you, among those born of women there has not risen one greater than John the Baptist; but he who is least in the kingdom of heaven is greater than he. And from the days of John the Baptist until now the kingdom of heaven suffers violence, and the violent take it by force. For all the prophets and the law prophesied until John. And if you are willing to receive it, he is Elijah who is to come. He who has ears to hear, let him hear!"* (Matthew 11:11–15)

Jesus sends John's disciples back to John with a simple message, a simple and deeply honest God Dare: Tell John what's happening here. Tell him miracles that no one has seen for *centuries* are happening every day! Tell him although it doesn't make sense and it may be impossible to understand why, I'm allowing you to perish in prison. . .but *don't doubt*. Take My dare to trust even when you don't comprehend. Trust until death. And if you can do that and not be offended because I didn't make things work out exactly as you'd hoped, you are blessed.

Sometimes God can seem mean and capricious or insensitive and uncaring, but He never is. Rest assured He always has a bigger plan in His mind than you can see. His perspective is so very different from ours and far beyond our finding out.

Some of you reading these words *will* be called as martyrs for your faith and witness. You may find yourselves in a foreign land that's hostile to the Gospel and dared by God to trust and believe in the face of certain death, *not* being set free at the eleventh hour of your trial. You may be called, like John the Baptist and Paul, Stephen and Peter, and so many more, to die for your faith. Will you let Jesus pick?

Scriptures to Think About

- *"Assuredly, I say to you, among those born of women there has not risen one greater than John the Baptist."* (Matthew 11:11)
- *"Chains and tribulations await me. But none of these things move me."* (Acts 20:23–24)
- *Now it came to pass, when Jesus finished commanding His twelve disciples, that He departed from there to teach and to preach in their cities. And when John had heard in prison about the works of Christ, he sent two of his disciples and said to Him, "Are You the Coming One, or do we look for another?" Jesus answered and said to them, "Go and tell John the things which you hear and see: The blind see and the lame walk; the lepers are cleansed and the deaf hear; the dead are raised up*

and the poor have the gospel preached to them. And blessed is he who is not offended because of Me." (Matthew 11:1–6)

- *I have been crucified with Christ; it is no longer I who live, but Christ lives in me; and the life which I now live in the flesh I live by faith in the Son of God, who loved me and gave Himself for me.* (Galatians 2:20)

- *"The Spirit of the Lord GOD is upon Me, because the LORD has anointed Me to preach good tidings to the poor; He has sent Me to heal the brokenhearted, to proclaim liberty to the captives, and the opening of the prison to those who are bound; to proclaim the acceptable year of the LORD, and the day of vengeance of our God; to comfort all who mourn, to console those who mourn in Zion, to give them beauty for ashes, the oil of joy for mourning, the garment of praise for the spirit of heaviness; that they may be called trees of righteousness, the planting of the LORD, that He may be glorified."* (Isaiah 61:1–3)

- *Then the eyes of the blind shall be opened, and the ears of the deaf shall be unstopped. Then the lame shall leap like a deer, and the tongue of the dumb sing. For waters shall burst forth in the wilderness, and streams in the desert. The parched ground shall become a pool, and the thirsty land springs of water.* (Isaiah 35:5–7)

God Dare Secrets

- God will dare some of us to die for Him.
- God's love doesn't separate God's children from difficulties.
- Suffering will reveal what's in our heart.
- Our only hope in tragic times is God's ever-present love.
- There's danger in speaking truth to power.

Discussion Questions

- Have you ever expected God to do something a certain way? What happened when He didn't?

- Are you accusing God of giving you snakes and stones? What do you need to do to see He's offering you bread and fish?

- Do you feel entitled to a certain kind of future? Why?

- Will you let offense halt your God Dare?

- Is your version of Christianity worth dying for?

- Will you give Him the means and manner of your death?

Chapter 12

THE MAIDSERVANT

I'm betting you could've heard a pin drop: all heaven holding their collective breath as Gabriel waited patiently for her response. Would she say yes? Would she politely but firmly demur? How would she handle the chance to make history, to change the world at its core, to shake up the very foundation on which she'd based her faith? Would she risk *everything* to take on God's will—her reputation, her life, her happiness?

She must've been terrified. I mean, imagine an angel, Gabriel no less, appearing right now in front of you. Holy smokes, it makes perfect sense the angels always say "Fear not" when they appear. *Of course* she would've been afraid!

We know she was young, likely about fifteen or so, but I doubt she was aware at the time she was "blessed and highly favored" among women. I love how God has adjectives describing us only He knows! An ordinary Jewish girl, betrothed to a hardworking, ordinary man, Mary finds herself thrust smack-dab into the midst of heaven's most extraordinary God Dare:

> *Then the angel said to her, "Do not be afraid, Mary, for you have found favor with God. And behold, you will conceive in your womb and bring forth a Son, and shall call His name Jesus. He will be great, and will be called the Son of the Highest; and the Lord God will give Him the throne of His father David. And He will reign over the house of Jacob*

forever, and of His kingdom there will be no end."
(Luke 1:30–33)

I'm sure Gabriel's words frightened and confused her—they would be difficult for anyone to fathom. I'm amazed she asked only one question! Can you imagine? I would have peppered Gabriel with a thousand questions. But simple, innocent Mary only asked one. And it made perfect sense since she was about to get married. "How can this be, since I do not know a man?" (Luke 1:34).

It's almost as if she heard nothing else the angel said after he told her she was going to "conceive in your womb and bring forth a Son." No questions about thrones or reigning or kingdoms. She heard the word *Son* and she wanted to know about *that*!

So Gabriel explained how it was going to happen. He explained the Holy Spirit will overshadow her and the Holy One who is born will be called the Son of God. He also let her know that her cousin Elizabeth, well past childbearing age, had conceived a child and was in her sixth month. For with God, he says, nothing is impossible.

I don't know how much of it she grasped in the moment, but, and this is my absolute favorite thing about Mary, even though she couldn't possibly understand the gravity of it all, she responded with pure, innocent, humble beauty. She heard the God Dare in the angel's astounding proposal. She could say no if she wanted to, free will and all, *but she didn't.* With words birthed from a heart steeped in humility, she speaks one of the most awe-inspiring declarations in all scripture. . .and I imagine all heaven holding their breath to hear her answer: " 'Behold the maidservant of the Lord! Let it be to me according to your word.' And the angel departed from her" (Luke 1:38).

She yielded her will, reason, and reputation because she knew her God, and she knew, by her obedience, He alone was responsible for the outcome. I imagine all heaven breathed a huge sigh of relief and great joy!

She had complete clarity about who she was: a maidservant. She knew who God was: the Lord, *her* Lord. And she knew He knew best. She agreed to have her world utterly upended as she said yes to rejection, to shunning, to a bad reputation, to possible divorce, to slander.

Did she have any idea the trouble it would cause, this God Dare she'd just agreed to? Did she realize Joseph might abandon her? Did she know she might be stoned to death? Maybe so, but it didn't matter. She knew beyond the shadow of a doubt, "He who is mighty has done great things for me and holy is His name" (Luke 1:49).

She trusted the Lord completely. If she was afraid, she decided to *do it afraid*. The God of the universe offered pure grace, and innocent Mary said *yes*. Mary believed. So she bungee jumped into a future and a God Dare that completely changed history for eternity. And this is the reason why: Mary was willing to make room.

When the angel came to her bringing the biggest God Dare of all time, she didn't hesitate. She made room. She opened her heart, her life, her future, and her womb and gave Him a place to grow. Joseph wasn't so sure. In fact, he wanted to "put her away secretly" (Matthew 1:19), and really, who could blame him? Looking at the situation from the outside, he had justification. But an angel appeared to Joseph in a dream and told him the baby in Mary's womb was holy, and his job was to marry her and call the child Jesus. It took an angel and a powerful dream to convince Joseph to make room, but eventually he did too. On a side note, did you notice how the angel doesn't tell Joseph the same things he tells Mary?

"But while he thought about these things, behold, an angel of the Lord appeared to him in a dream, saying, 'Joseph, son of David, do not be afraid to take to you Mary your wife, for that which is conceived in her is of the Holy Spirit. And she will bring forth a Son, and you shall call His name Jesus, for He will save His people from their sins'" (Matthew 1:20–21). The angel never mentioned David or thrones or kingdoms. He simply told Joseph not to be afraid, take Mary as his wife, name the baby Jesus, and He will save His people from their sins. Gabriel didn't bother to mention Jesus was the Son of God. A pretty important detail, don't you think? I wonder why.

If I were trying to convince a man of something, I would tell him all the incredible reasons why he should say yes. But Joseph gets a lot less information than Mary does. And Mary didn't even seem to hear all the awesome things Gabriel spoke. She wanted to know how on earth she would be able to have a baby since she was a virgin!

Of all the ways He could have entered the world, who would have dreamed of sending a helpless baby to ordinary, un-royal, unremarkable parents? It made absolutely no sense. God, the Word, the Creator of the universe, bigger than galaxies, the One in whom everything holds together, reduces Himself to a tiny cluster of cells in a young woman's womb. The Word becomes a wee bit of flesh. The greatest of all becomes the least of these, delivered in blood and water in a humble stable. All because a young woman with a pure heart said yes to the God Dare. All because Mary was willing to make room.

Scriptures to Think About

- *Then Mary said, "Behold the maidservant of the Lord! Let it be to me according to your word." And the angel departed from her.* (Luke 1:38)

- *"He who is mighty has done great things for me, and holy is His name."* (Luke 1:49)

- *Then the angel said to her, "Do not be afraid, Mary, for you have found favor with God. And behold, you will conceive in your womb and bring forth a Son, and shall call His name JESUS. He will be great, and will be called the Son of the Highest; and the Lord God will give Him the throne of His father David. And He will reign over the house of Jacob forever, and of His kingdom there will be no end." (Luke 1:30–33)*

God Dare Secrets

- The God Dare comes to those willing to make room.
- God will use ordinary humans to do extraordinary exploits.
- God has specific adjectives He uses to describe you.

Discussion Questions

- Will you yield your will, your reason, and your reputation if God asks you to? Why or why not?

- What distractions can you remove to make room for God?

- Do you think you're too young to accomplish anything for God? Based on what?

- Are you willing to make room even when you don't fully comprehend what God is asking you to do?

Chapter 13

THE WEALTHY SHEPHERD

We were in the car driving home. As I read the first sentence of the email, I inhaled so sharply at the shocking words I scared my poor husband to death! It was completely involuntary because the news was that difficult. I sat stunned and heartbroken at the words, not even knowing how to respond. I had no touchstone for this.

I assumed I knew God's ways, but I could not fathom how this happened. There was so much prayer and faith, so much *belief.* My friend was in the middle of a desperate and difficult trial. One of her children had a critical medical issue and the diagnosis and treatment were as heart wrenching as any family should ever have to endure. This child's life had been spared, but the family's future forever altered. I'd been praying along with many others and believing for months that God, in His mercy, would provide a miracle and wonderful testimony for this family.

But God, in His mercy, didn't. Sometimes God allows in His wisdom what He can prevent with His power to bring about an even greater good in the future. This family walked the path of what looked like irretrievable tragedy. As I pondered the heartbreaking situation, questions poured into my brain. Why are our lives allowed to be devastated sometimes? Is God really merciful, or do I just not recognize His mercy when it's most severe? Romans 11:33 says: "How unsearchable are His judgments and His ways past finding out!"

In my life, I have had my own times when I felt God was completely unsearchable, and I couldn't begin to fathom His judgments. These were times when He seemed unrelentingly hard and mean and utterly unmerciful. I'm ashamed to admit how many nights, during my desperate years of wanting more children, I tiptoed out of the bedroom to head into a room across the house and cry my eyes out, yelling at God: "What I want is good! You know I'll raise any child You give me to love You!" "How could You, God? I thought You were merciful and just! You're supposed to be a good Father, but You don't seem good to me *at all*."

I'm a little embarrassed now to publicly admit my atrocious attitude, but at the time, I simply couldn't see why He wouldn't give Mike and me more children. I didn't know He was already preparing our daughter for the life He was calling her to; the reality of that hadn't yet appeared on our radar screen. It's clear to me now, years later, that she needed our complete attention to walk fully into her calling, but neither of us could see it back then.

When His Greatest Mercy Is Wrapped in His Deepest Test

Eventually, I released my bitterness against God as I realized the hard way that His ways are not my ways, and that His ways are much higher than mine. His mercy seemed mighty severe at the time and not much like mercy at all, but when the dust settled and the fog lifted and the years passed, it was easy to see it is *indeed* mercy. Just not in its nice Sunday wrapping. He transformed our understanding of mercy, and we learned His greatest mercy is sometimes wrapped in His deepest test.

Here's what I know about mercy:

- Mercy has a bigger purpose than our happiness.
- Mercy has a plan.
- Mercy makes itself plain in time.
- Mercy is misunderstood.

When trials come that devastate, we can't see the mercy, only the devastation. We can't see God in it, but I promise you, He is there. His mercy is real, and no matter what we go through, eventually we *will* see His hand.

I know mercy is in the trial my friend is going through right now. She can't see it through the severity, the finality, the utter heartbreak, but I'm praying she will. I'm praying that one day she'll see that in His tender mercy, God allowed what He could have prevented because of a future good she can't see right now. He always has the bigger picture in mind. He sees the end from the beginning, and if He allows it I can only, like Job, bow in worship and remember that in it all, He is not after my happiness but my highest good.

Admit it, Job is the one character we *all* wish was not in the Bible. We don't even want to consider his fate falling to us, in fact, don't even go there. It's a hard story with hard truth and some of it is hard to grasp. But the God Dare is in the Job story too.

Job was one of the biblical good guys—in fact he was "blameless and upright, and one who feared God and shunned evil" (Job 1:1).

This description likely befits most of you reading this book. You too are good, right? You don't watch R-rated movies or gamble your money away, or drink beer all day, and you shun evil too, right? Job had no hidden or besetting sin in his life that we're aware of. The primary quality setting him apart was his *righteousness*. Like I said, he was a good guy.

For the record, I don't believe in luck or fate. I absolutely believe in the sovereignty of an almighty God. I don't believe God is capable of causing evil, ever. It's not even remotely possible. God *is* love. He is light, and in Him there is no darkness at all. He is holy, pure, and powerful, and He has plans and purposes, ways and means far beyond finding out, certainly beyond my understanding. His ways are higher than mine, and although I don't always like His choices for my life, I accept them. . .albeit sometimes reluctantly. I've given up making it my job to try to figure out why God does what He does or why He lets bad things happen to good people. But I'm utterly convinced of this: sometimes God allows in His wisdom what He could prevent by His power for future glory.

I'm not a theologian, and this book is certainly not a treatise on faith or sovereignty. Instead, it is merely my best effort to share thoughts and what I've observed in my life, my friends' lives, and what I've gleaned from studying the Word of God these many years. It is not my job to try to figure Him out, nor is it yours. My job, and this is the scary part (at least for me), is to trust and obey no matter what comes. Whatever He allows, in His wisdom, to come into my life, even if it shatters my concept of Him. *Especially* if it shatters my small, narrow concept of Him, I've learned to simply trust Him.

So, back to Job. . .not only was he righteous, he was rich. I mean, really filthy stinkin' rich! He was blessed with ten children, thousands of animals, and a large household. In fact, the Bible tells us Job was the greatest of all the people of the east. Job was rich, righteous, and famous. Probably popular and good looking too, *People* magazine's Sexiest Man Alive maybe, but who knows? All we know is Job had it all. He was blessed and highly favored. However, Job had a little issue with fear. God knew it and *Satan did too*. "For the thing I greatly feared has come upon me, and what I dreaded has happened to me" (Job 3:25).

Here's the tricky part. God, in His divine wisdom, allowed Job to be tested. He allowed Job to go through hell and back to establish the fact that Job *really was* a righteous man. But God knew Job needed a deep revelation of God's purposes and a deeper understanding of his own nature. Through testing, Job gained those things and so much more. Through perseverance, Job would learn God was compassionate and merciful, not cruel and capricious.

The Bible informs us how one day Satan appeared before God

after he had walked to and fro on the earth, and he and God had a little conversation. I'm absolutely fascinated by this: after clearly noticing all the blessing and protection in Job's life, Satan didn't point Job out to God and ask God if he could test him, no. *God pointed Job out to Satan.* And He knew exactly what He was doing. He dangled the bait right in front of the devil, and the devil bit.

> *Then the LORD said to Satan,* **"Have you considered My servant Job, that there is none like him on the earth, a blameless and upright man, one who fears God and shuns evil?"** *So Satan answered the LORD and said, "Does Job fear God for nothing? Have You not made a hedge around him, around his household, and around all that he has on every side? You have blessed the work of his hands, and his possessions have increased in the land. But now, stretch out Your hand and touch all that he has, and he will surely curse You to Your face!" And the LORD said to Satan, "Behold, all that he has is in your power; only do not lay a hand on his person."* (Job 1:8–12, emphasis added)

So God allowed Job to lose everything. *Everything*—including his children, all ten, killed in one day from a violent storm. Most of his animals stolen by raiders and the rest burned up by fire from heaven. *All in the same day.* And Job, who had every right to be angry with God, instead of lashing out and impeaching God's goodness, says these infamous words after he shaved his head, fell to the ground, and worshipped: " 'Naked I came from my mother's womb, and naked shall I return there. The LORD gave, and the LORD has taken away; blessed be the name of the LORD.' In all this Job did not sin nor charge God with wrong" (Job 1:21–22).

Satan offered a potent devil's dare in removing every single thing in Job's life that brought joy and peace and fulfillment. He removed it all in a single stroke, because he fully expected Job to curse God to His face. We all know God has a plan for our lives, but here's a newsflash: Satan does too. God, who created Job and knew him intimately, dared Job to come out into the deeper deeps of loss and grief, sorrow and suffering, and choose to trust anyway. And because He knew Job far better than Satan did, God knew exactly how Job would react.

I get it. God is sovereign and He reveals Himself when He takes us through trials. As He reveals Himself we see Him more clearly, and the more clearly we see Him, the more we can love Him. It isn't easy, and although I didn't go through anything nearly as difficult as Job, going through infertility was my Waterloo. My God Dare and devil's dare all wrapped up in one big, heart-altering trial. I know my trial is hardly comparable to Job's, but it's the hardest thing I've ever gone through.

Why would God allow someone to suffer an accident and go through life paralyzed? Why would He allow children to be born with a life-threatening disease, or Down syndrome, or autism? Why would He allow a frightening diagnosis to fall in your lap? Why did He allow your marriage to fall apart? Why would He allow a thousand and one difficulties to enter in, strangling your faith and destroying your joy?

The Deeper Deeps

God draws us out into what I call "the deeper deeps," into the fellowship of His sufferings, to humble us and allow us to discover *He is enough*. God truly loved Job, and because He cared for him so much He spoke directly to Job out of the whirlwind. Here's my theory: God brought Job to the end of himself so he could find his *everything* in God alone.

I believe with all my heart God's will for us is *always* good. There are times and seasons of testing for each of us. One big overarching God Dare is this: When life falls apart will you trust Him or curse Him? When God says no to the thing you want—the baby, the spouse, the job, the good diagnosis, the career—will you still love Him? Will you let Him humble you and be your El Shaddai, your Almighty? Can you trust in knowing He required the same of His Son?

Faith is the doorway into trust. It's the certainty God will never leave me or forsake me because He loves me! It's being certain, whatever circumstances I'm in, that He knows and He cares. Like Job said, "Though He slay me, yet will I trust Him" (Job 13:15).

The only way you know if you have faith is when the trial comes. The loss, the illness, the tragedy, the thing bringing you to the end of yourself and the beginning of Him. Then how do you know if your faith is growing or real?

You. Stand.

When you've done all, stand. Stand therefore. Stand and fight because faith is a walk, but it's a battle too. It gets hard and sweaty and bloody, but the fruit will be a faith that actually moves mountains and changes the world. Faith is a gift, and we can ask for more. Countless times I've prayed, "I believe, Lord. Help my unbelief." I have a measure but not the fullness of faith. But I'm still believing for impossible things, big things, God things only He can do. I'm walking and fighting and sometimes barely standing, but I press on. Join me, won't you?

James 5:11 says this about Job: "Indeed we count them blessed who endure. You have heard of the perseverance of Job and seen the end intended by the Lord—that the Lord is very compassionate and merciful."

God wanted Job to *see* and to *know* who He is. All along God had an "intended end" for Job. He knew Job would come forth as gold, and Job would ultimately understand God and see His mercy and compassion.

There have been seasons in life when I thought God was *anything* but compassionate or merciful. In fact, for a while there I thought He hated me because of my wretched past, and I was convinced He had it out for me and I couldn't understand Him at all. I nearly gave up and gave in to the devil's dare, and the world would have applauded my decision. But I chose to let Him draw me into the deeper deeps, that fearful place of trust and acceptance, the place where you can't feel your feet on the sandy ocean bottom, the place of not knowing and trusting anyway. He is God and I am not, and He alone knows the end from the beginning. He loves me, and His will for me, His thoughts toward me, His plans for me, and for you too, dear reader, are always, *always* good.

I have a dear friend who's walked through an exhausting year of testing. First she received an unnerving cancer diagnosis. Next she began chemo and lost all her hair. Then her husband went through a debilitating health crisis. As if that's not enough, they almost lost their house but were able to sell it in the nick of time. Their health, home, livelihood, and finances all hit in one year. If anyone I know had reasons to curse God, my friend did.

Yet in spite of her severe trials or maybe because of them, her faith has grown more resolute. She's a shining beacon of steadfast hope in the Lord to all who know her. In the face of overwhelming trials that would do most of us in, she stands strong in her faith because she knows her God. She's taken the God Dare to trust the light when all she can see is darkness. She believes in the goodness of God as the chemo drips into her arm and she wants to throw up. She praises His name as she walks away from the house where she raised her family. She's been deeply humbled, and though she can't tell you why she's facing such unrelenting trials, she knows God in His sovereignty has allowed it. And she's okay with it. She's being tried in the furnace of His testing, and she's coming forth as gold.

Everyone around her knows it and is amazed and inspired by her faith.

As for Job, after God spoke to him from the whirlwind, Job responded with deep humility. "I have heard of You by the hearing of the ear, but now my eye sees You. Therefore I abhor myself, and repent in dust and ashes" (Job 42:5–6).

God dares Job one last time. He tells Job to intercede for his three friends—the friends that had given him deeply flawed counsel—because our intercession, especially for those who have done us wrong, brings restoration. God spoke directly to Eliphaz the Temanite, one of the three "friends" of Job: "My wrath is aroused against you and your two friends, for you have not spoken of Me what is right, as My servant Job has" (Job 42:7).

When God dares us to intercede for others, our intercession turns everything around. "And the LORD restored Job's losses when he prayed for his friends" (Job 42:10).

Job had heard of and known *about* God, but now God has revealed Himself to Job. Finally, Job *sees*, and all he can do is repent. Everything the devil tried to do by destroying his family and possessions and causing grave sickness is all reversed as Job intercedes in obedience. And ultimately God restores Job giving him back twice as much as he had before.

Now the LORD blessed the latter days of Job more than his beginning; for he had fourteen thousand sheep, six thousand camels, one thousand yoke of oxen, and one thousand female donkeys. He also had seven sons and three daughters. . . . In all the land were found no women so beautiful as the daughters of Job; and their father gave them an inheritance among their brothers. After this Job lived one hundred and forty years, and saw his children and grandchildren for four generations. So Job died, old and full of days. (Job 42:12–13, 15–17)

At the beginning of his trials, Job *worships*. At the end, he *repents*. What a model for our lives. What a hero of faith is Job! F. B. Meyer says, "It is one thing to hear of God, another to see and know Him close at hand. Well may we loathe our proud words and repent in dust and ashes."[8]

God's ways are higher than mine. I know God doesn't go about killing children and animals and causing us to become sick. But when trials devastate, when God allows in His wisdom what He could prevent with His power, we can take the God Dare and persevere because we know His character and because, at the end of the trial if we stand firm and faithful, *we too will see God*.

One fascinating thought: Job's wife had ten children at the beginning. Even though she tells Job to "curse God and die" (Job 2:9), nothing is ever mentioned about her again. However, the Bible tells us Job has ten more children in his latter days with no mention of a new wife. Does that mean his unnamed wife had twenty babies? Ladies, can you even imagine?

Scriptures to Think About

- *"Naked I came from my mother's womb, and naked shall I return there. The LORD gave, and the LORD has taken away; blessed be the name of the LORD." In all this Job did not sin nor charge God with wrong.* (Job 1:21–22)
- *Indeed we count them blessed who endure. You have heard of the perseverance of Job and seen the end intended by the Lord— that the Lord is very compassionate and merciful.* (James 5:11)
- *"I have heard of You by the hearing of the ear, but now my eye sees You. Therefore I abhor myself, and repent in dust and ashes."* (Job 42:5–6)
- *This light momentary affliction is preparing for us an eternal weight of glory beyond all comparison, as we look not to*

---

[8] F. B. Meyer, *Devotional Commentary*.

the things that are seen but to the things that are unseen.
(2 Corinthians 4:17–18 ESV)

- *Not that I speak in regard to need, for I have learned in whatever state I am, to be content: I know how to be abased, and I know how to abound. Everywhere and in all things I have learned both to be full and to be hungry, both to abound and to suffer need. I can do all things through Christ who strengthens me.* (Philippians 4:11–13)

- *That I may know Him and the power of His resurrection, and the fellowship of His sufferings, being conformed to His death.* (Philippians 3:10)

- *And the LORD restored Job's losses when he prayed for his friends.* (Job 42:10)

God Dare Secrets

- God will allow in His wisdom what He could prevent by His power to allow a greater future good.
- God's greatest mercy is sometimes wrapped in His deepest test.
- God didn't promise us a life without struggle. Triumph follows our trials if we press in to Him.
- Suffering reveals what's in our hearts.
- God uses suffering *in* our lives to make Jesus known *through* our lives.
- How you respond to suffering may determine how others respond to the Lord.
- If you want to truly know God, He will take you into the deep place of suffering and sorrow.
  - Intercession can turn your circumstances around.
  - Affliction brings us into the fellowship of Christ's suffering.
  - Your deepest pain is holy ground.
  - Jesus beckons to us in the broken places of our lives.

Discussion Questions

- Has God allowed you to be deeply tested? How?

- If God took away something you treasure, would He still be enough?

- Are you willing to enter into the fellowship of His sufferings to know Him better? If not, why not?

- When life falls apart, will you still trust Him?

- Has God brought you to the end of your strength? Have you discovered He is enough?

- Are you willing to go with God into the deeper deeps of suffering and sorrow?

- Are you willing to suffer well?

- Will you intercede for the ones who've given you bad counsel? The ones who've hurt and offended you?

Chapter 14

THE BARREN WIFE

I endured a lot of pain, guilt, and heartache during my years of infertility, longing for something I couldn't have no matter how much I wanted it. But to be totally honest, I did *not* suffer well during those years. I sulked, complained, and felt sorry for myself, and I yelled at God more than once.

When our daughter was eighteen months old, I suffered an ectopic or tubal pregnancy. I miscarried the baby, nearly died, and ended up in the hospital for four days. I survived the miscarriage, but my desire for a houseful of children did not. Three adoption attempts fell through, and my fertility treatments utterly failed.

Misery became my constant companion. My suffering drove me into deep depression, so I well understand Hannah's desperation in 1 Samuel 1:1–28. As I grew in knowing who God *is*, I began to see that in spite of—or more likely because of—my suffering, I saw my faith grow as I sought God more deeply than ever before. I began to understand why He allowed me to be so miserable. I didn't realize I was *choosing* misery. Ingratitude distinguished my life, filling me with despair. What I didn't have consumed my thoughts, and I ignored the profound blessings right in front of me.

In Hebrews 5:8 (ESV) it says of Jesus: "Although he was a son, he learned obedience from what he suffered." There's a purpose for our pain, even when we can't see it. Let me give you some hope right now if you're in the middle of a trial causing deep suffering. Time gives perspective. As the years go by, if you continue to seek God in the middle of your trial, you *will* begin to see the ways and whys of God. The only antidote to discouragement I've found is this: tell God how you really feel, and leave your problem in His hands.

God gave us one child because the one He gave us had a big purpose, and she needed our full attention. In spite of my abortion years earlier, He allowed ordinary us to raise an extraordinary child, one whose destiny proved real and profound. He also likely knew we could only handle one child, even though our hearts' desire was a houseful.

As I grow and go on with God, He gently guides and teaches, and as I listen and follow, my clenched hands gently open, and what I grasp tight He teaches me to *give*. He brought this home in a profound way years ago and I've never forgotten the lesson. It's this: *just because a blessing falls into your lap doesn't mean it's always yours to keep.*

I've never shared this particular story until now. But it's pressing hard on my heart, so maybe someone needs to hear it. In fact, I wasn't going to put this story in my book, but here goes.

There are times when it looks like your dream has come true, but you come to find it's not actually for you. You've been chosen to be the conduit, the channel of blessing in another's life. It's not an easy lesson but one we'll all be taught if we want to go deep with God. Here's how it happened for my husband Mike and me.

Twenty years ago, Mike and I were still in the throes of raising our young daughter. We'd moved to Florida a couple years earlier, and after battling infertility and three failed adoption attempts, we got it into our thick heads we would be raising an only child. We took a financial freedom class at our church and became friends with another couple who were in our exact same circumstances— raising one daughter and unable to have more children.

At the same time, other good friends of ours were in Hungary adopting a baby girl. They too had waited years for their dream to come true, and we were thrilled for them. They were finally going to have a baby in their arms! One evening, the phone rang and it was our friends, in Hungary, calling us. They were excited to share how everything was moving smoothly with the adoption. Then they drop this bombshell. They tell us there's a young, unmarried woman who's about to have a baby, a boy (my dream), and she's placing him for adoption and looking for an American family. *They tell us he's our baby if we want him.*

Oh, how my mama-heart leaped in that moment! My hopes and dreams coming true in one phone call! Except right in that moment I heard the Lord say this deep in my spirit, and Mike, on the other line, heard the exact same thing:

"That's not your baby."

Wait. What? Are you sure, Lord? I've been waiting a long time for this!

"That's not your baby."

I don't usually hear God's voice so clearly in my spirit. There are a few times I have, like the time I heard Him tell me to write my first book. *When I do hear Him, it's always life changing.*

"That's not your baby."

And I knew it was true. I knew this baby was the son our friends from church had been praying for. God let our biggest blessing become our deepest test.

We hung up the phone and I shared what I was sensing with Mike, and he felt exactly the same way. So we called our friends from church and told them the news, connected them with our friends in Hungary, and soon after they went and got their son. *Just because a blessing falls into your lap doesn't always mean it's yours to keep.*

A few months later they dedicated their son at church, and Mike and I were on the platform as part of the celebration. I looked at this beautiful child, this perfect baby boy, this answer to prayer, and it broke me. It was so hard but so right. Harder than almost anything I've ever done. I cried a lot that day, but God assured me over and over it was *right*. Doing the right thing doesn't mean it won't be hard. *It will be very hard.* Sometimes gut-wrenchingly hard.

If I'd simply trusted in my feelings or followed my heart, I never would have given that baby up. But feelings and emotions lie. My heart, and yours too, is not to be trusted. The world tells us to follow our hearts, but God says something altogether different: "The heart is deceitful above all things and desperately wicked; who can know it?" (Jeremiah 17:9).

My heart has deceived me countless times, usually with something good I can justify. But good is the enemy of the best *every time*. Jesus wasn't led by His feelings; He only ever did and said what He saw the Father doing or heard Him saying.

> *"Most assuredly, I say to you, the Son can do nothing of Himself, but what He sees the Father do; for whatever He does, the Son also does in like manner."* (John 5:19)

> *"For I have not spoken on My own authority; but the Father who sent Me gave Me a command, what I should say and what I should speak."* (John 12:49)

I'm learning to lay down my feelings for the joy of living a Spirit-led life! It says in Romans 8:14: "For as many as are led by the Spirit of God, these are sons of God." Sonship speaks of maturity and authority, two things I desperately need.

You know, as I get older, I really want God to take me into the deep place of knowing Him. It's far better to partake in the "fellowship of His sufferings" (Philippians 3:10), because only through the doorway of His cross can we experience the power of His resurrection. It's all about love in the end, our willingness to be broken bread and poured-out wine in another's life, our willingness to become a channel of blessing to bring someone else's dream to pass.

Following Jesus and letting go of our feelings will cost us, but in the end aren't we called to relinquish our right to be right? Our right to *have* rights? We get the chance every so often to leave the fragrance of Christ behind us.

Jesus Christ alone can transform my deceitful and wicked heart into a channel of love and blessing and a spring of living water. He alone can give me the desire of my heart and then ask me to give it away. And when I do, I become more like Him.

Hannah illustrates one of the best examples of suffering well and allowing her life to be a channel of blessing for another, in all of scripture. To refresh the story, Hannah was the first wife of Elkanah, and she lived during the time of the Judges in Israel. Hannah enjoyed the position of the favored first wife, but she could not conceive. In fact, 1 Samuel 1:5 says "the LORD had closed her womb." But as you'll see, He closed her womb for a purpose—because sometimes the barren tree yields the richest fruit.

Hannah's rival, wife number two named Peninnah, had no trouble popping out baby after baby and provoking Hannah relentlessly for *years*. Let's pick up the story in 1 Samuel:

> *So it was, year by year, when she went up to the house of the LORD, that she provoked her; therefore, she wept and did not eat.*
>
> *Then Elkanah her husband said to her, "Hannah, why do you weep? Why do you not eat? And why is your heart grieved? Am I not better to you than ten sons?"*
>
> *So Hannah arose after they had finished eating and drinking in Shiloh. Now Eli the priest was sitting on the seat by the doorpost of the tabernacle of the LORD. And she*

was in bitterness of soul, and prayed to the LORD and wept in anguish. Then she made a vow and said, "O LORD of hosts, if You will indeed look on the affliction of Your maidservant and remember me, and not forget Your maidservant, but will give Your maidservant a male child, then I will give him to the LORD all the days of his life, and no razor shall come upon his head."

And it happened, as she continued praying before the LORD, that Eli watched her mouth. Now Hannah spoke in her heart; only her lips moved, but her voice was not heard. Therefore Eli thought she was drunk. So Eli said to her, "How long will you be drunk? Put your wine away from you!"

But Hannah answered and said, "No, my lord, I am a woman of sorrowful spirit. I have drunk neither wine nor intoxicating drink, but have poured out my soul before the LORD. Do not consider your maidservant a wicked woman, for out of the abundance of my complaint and grief I have spoken until now." Then Eli answered and said, "Go in peace, and the God of Israel grant your petition which you have asked of Him." And she said, "Let your maidservant find favor in your sight." So the woman went her way and ate, and her face was no longer sad. (1 Samuel 1:7–18)

There are so many things to deeply admire and love about Hannah. First, she took her complaint privately to God. She didn't chastise Peninnah or gossip about her or complain to her husband or harangue the priest. Pain became her catalyst to pray. Hannah could have retaliated, she could have despaired, she could have given up. But instead she prayed, she trusted, she believed. She took her pain directly to the Lord and then made an incredible vow, a vow to return the child she so desperately desired to the Lord if He would only answer her prayer.

Maybe that's exactly what God was waiting for! Hannah's unrelenting pain acted as the catalyst that pushed her to pray a secret, daring, audacious, and holy prayer. It's interesting to note she wept and prayed silently in a time in history when silent prayer was quite uncommon. The court of the tabernacle had many people coming and going, and Hannah had no choice but to pour out her heart in silent and tearful supplication.

I'm convinced Hannah's enduring faith enabled her to believe God heard every word of her anguished prayer. Desperation drove her to pray a completely *unselfish* prayer. She chose to believe and trust the Lord *before* her circumstances changed. Hannah knew her God more intimately than Eli, the priest, as he saw her lips move and thought she was drunk. He superficially saw but he didn't discern. It tells a lot about the state of worship in those days if people went into the house of the Lord drunk.

It's remarkable she never took revenge on Peninnah, wife number two, and didn't react in anger when falsely accused of being drunk by Eli, the priest. She suffered in silence, poured her heart out to the Lord, believed *before* she received, and ended up giving birth to Samuel, whose very name means, "God has heard." When Eli the priest blessed her and prayed for her and asked the Lord to grant her request, her outlook on life completely changed, well before her circumstances did. *Selah.*

Through a weak and undiscerning priest God dared Hannah to believe, and believe she did. Sarah, Rachel, and Hannah all desperately desired to have a child, but of the three, only Hannah went to the Lord in prayer. Both Eli and her husband misunderstood Hannah. How often does that cause us to become bitter, hopeless, or vindictive? Hannah became none of those things but instead poured out her request to God, and He tenderly answered her secret, holy prayer.

I find it incredible, of all the women mentioned in the Old Testament, Hannah is the only one who made a vow to the Lord and actually fulfilled it! After weaning Samuel, Hannah returns to Shiloh and hands her young son over to the priest knowing she will only see him once every year. She returns to God the very gift He gave her, the one thing she desired most, pouring out her heart in a beautiful song of worship, reminiscent of Mary's song of praise, the Magnificat. Incredibly, Hannah rejoices in God even *more* than in the gift of her son. In her time of releasing her precious son, dear Hannah offers her beautiful song to the Lord:

> *"My heart rejoices in the* Lord*; my horn is exalted in the* Lord*. I smile at my enemies, because I rejoice in Your salvation.*
>
> *"No one is holy like the* Lord*, for there is none besides You, nor is there any rock like our God. Talk no more so very proudly; let no arrogance come from your mouth,* [I'm pretty sure that's aimed right at Peninnah!] *for the* Lord *is the God of knowledge; and by Him actions are weighed.* [He sees you, wife number 2.]
>
> *"The bows of the mighty men are broken, and those who stumbled are girded with strength. Those who were full have hired themselves out for bread, and the hungry have ceased to hunger. Even the barren has borne seven, and she who has many children has become feeble.* [Take that, Peninnah!]
>
> *"The* Lord *kills and makes alive; He brings down to the grave and brings up. The* Lord *makes poor and makes rich; He brings low and lifts up. He raises the poor from the dust and lifts the beggar from the ash heap, to set them among princes and make them inherit the throne of glory.*
>
> *"For the pillars of the earth are the* Lord*'s, and He has set the world upon them.*
>
> *He will guard the feet of His saints, but the wicked shall be silent in darkness.*

"For by strength no man shall prevail. [I hope you're hearing me, Peninnah!] *The adversaries of the LORD shall be broken in pieces; from heaven He will thunder against them. The LORD will judge the ends of the earth. He will give strength to His king, and exalt the horn of His anointed."*
(1 Samuel 2:1–10)

How fitting righteous Samuel becomes the prophet chosen by God to bridge the bloody era between the judges and the kings of Israel, and the one God chose to anoint both Saul and David as the first two kings of Israel. Also, how fitting that Hannah's story includes giving birth to three sons and two daughters, but Peninnah is never mentioned again! Peninnah tried her hardest to bring Hannah low, but God exalted Hannah and made her promised son one of the greatest and most renowned men in the history of Israel.

Are there God Dares that arrive in answer to our desperation? Is God still looking for desperate ones with destinies yet to be realized to raise up a great man or woman? Trials come, and they can devastate our hope until we can no longer see His mercy through our devastation. Even if we can't see God, He is there. He feels everything we feel, and He sees every single tear. Even in my own struggle with infertility, I learned that His ways are not my ways, but they are much higher than mine. His mercy may have seemed severe at the time, but now I see clearly His mercy is real.

Scriptures to Think About

- *Although he was a son, he learned obedience through what he suffered.* (Hebrews 5:8 ESV)
- *"For the eyes of the LORD run to and fro throughout the whole earth, to show Himself strong on behalf of those whose heart is loyal to Him."* (2 Chronicles 16:9)
- *"Sing, O barren, you who have not borne! Break forth into*

singing, and cry aloud, you who have not labored with child!
For more are the children of the desolate than the children of the
married woman," says the LORD. *"Enlarge the place of your tent,*
and let them stretch out the curtains of your dwellings; do not
spare; lengthen your cords, and strengthen your stakes. For you
shall expand to the right and to the left, and your descendants
will inherit the nations, and make the desolate cities inhabited."
(Isaiah 54:1–3)

God Dare Secrets

- Barrenness always has a purpose.
- It's in the season of barrenness that we should sing.
- The richest fruit comes from the barren tree.
- Time gives perspective.
- It's easy to see and not discern.
- God hears every silent prayer we pray.
- At times God will dare you to believe *before* your circumstances change.
- Often our pain and desperation are the catalyst we need to pray.

Discussion Questions

- When your circumstances are desperate, is prayer your first line of defense? Why or why not?

- Do you believe God always hears your prayers?

- Has your pain ever been the catalyst to pray a secret, daring, holy prayer?

- Is prayer your first option or last resort?

- Are you willing to suffer well?

- Are you choosing misery or choosing to trust?

- Do you believe barrenness has a purpose?

- In your time of releasing what's most precious to you, can you worship? Will you?

- Will you pray a big, audacious prayer?

- Is it possible Hannah's plea and promise to God laid the foundation for the anointing on Samuel's life? How so?

- If God asks you to, are you willing to relinquish the very thing you most desperately want? What is it?

Chapter 15

THE DISOBEDIENT PROPHET

Sometimes we don't obey God because what He asks seems crazy and we don't have nearly the imagination to see everything He's already lined up. He tells us to *go* and we resist to the point of disobedience, which can lead to disastrous consequences. And to be perfectly honest, we just don't want to see God offer mercy to those we don't think deserve it. (Kind of like our current political climate. Am I right?)

Enter Jonah, whose name means "the dove," a bona fide prophet and likely a disciple of Elijah. Jewish tradition suggests he was the promised son of the widow of Zarephath, whose birth Elijah prophesied and who, years later, God restored to life. (See 1 Kings 17:8–24.)

Jonah is the *only* prophet in the Old Testament sent to preach a message of repentance and mercy to a Gentile nation. He's also the only prophet to attempt to flee from God's presence. Can you hear the God Dare in this scripture?

> *Now the word of the LORD came to Jonah the son of Amittai, saying,* **"Arise, go to Nineveh, that great city, and cry out against it; for their wickedness has come up before Me."** *But Jonah arose to flee to Tarshish from the presence of the LORD. He went down to Joppa, and found a ship going to Tarshish; so he paid the fare, and went down into it, to go with them to Tarshish from the presence of the LORD.*
> (Jonah 1:1–3, emphasis added)

As long as Jonah could be a prophet in the place and in the way he *wanted* to be a prophet, he was in. As soon as God required him to do something he didn't want to do, he tried to check out. *But God.* Sometimes God will make us take a God Dare even when we try to run from it!

God was inviting Jonah into His great story, His commission an invitation to go to an unsaved people group and offer them the opportunity to repent. But Jonah didn't see it as an invitation, instead more like a huge disruption. How could he have known God was giving him the opportunity to be involved in one of the greatest revivals in history? He couldn't possibly have known that his story would be shared by Jesus Himself as an example centuries later: "The men of Nineveh will rise up in the judgment with this generation and condemn it, for they repented at the preaching of Jonah; and indeed a greater than Jonah is here" (Luke 11:32).

But think about this for a minute. "The word of the LORD came to Jonah. . ." What a commission, what an honor! God actually *spoke* to him. Obviously, Jonah had something going for him, except for the fear thing. Jonah knew the Lord, but he didn't quite get what God's mercy was all about.

Jonah didn't want to go. In fact, he *wanted* to see the people of Nineveh, the capital of Assyria (called "the city of blood" in the book of Nahum), wiped out, not offered mercy or the opportunity to repent. In fact, Jonah utterly despised those people. He was prejudiced and dare I say racist in his attitude toward the Ninevites. Oh, how little we understand God's great mercy and love for *all* people! And how little we understand God alone is in control of the destiny of all nations.

In Jonah 1:2 God told Jonah to "arise, go to Nineveh, that great city, and cry out against it; for their wickedness has come up before Me."

And Jonah indeed arose—except he fled in the exact opposite

direction, to Tarshish to be exact. He knew the bloody reputation of the Ninevites, a people so evil they would fix the heads of their conquered enemies on the city walls to make sure you knew just how fierce they were. I might flee in the opposite direction too!

So Jonah boards a boat heading to Tarshish, then immediately heads down to the lowest part of the ship and promptly falls asleep. He totally interrupts God's plan, comfortable in his disobedience—so comfortable in fact, he falls asleep and stays asleep as a wild storm begins to rage.

I see so much of myself in Jonah, the fear part mostly. It's always scary when God dares us to do a possibly life-threatening thing, like going to Nineveh—the most powerful and wicked city in the known world—inhabited by the hated and feared Assyrians. The Assyrians despised the Israelites and destroyed entire people groups, and Jonah knew this. Going to their city to preach repentance and knowing he would likely be killed would terrify anyone. So Jonah takes the cowardly devil's dare and flees.

Jonah knew this truth about God, that He is a "gracious God and merciful, slow to anger and abounding in steadfast love" (Jonah 4:2 ESV).

But there were a few things about the Ninevites Jonah *didn't* know. The perimeter of Nineveh was seven miles and the walls around the city were wide enough for three chariots to ride abreast. Jonah didn't know Nineveh had suffered two plagues from 765 BC to 759 BC. He also didn't know they had experienced a frightening total eclipse of the sun in 763 BC, terrifying the inhabitants. Jonah had no idea God was preparing the Ninevites for a great revival; he only knew of their bloody reputation. And when God directed him to go preach a message of repentance to a people he abhorred, his fear and hatred drove him in the exact opposite direction.

Jonah took the devil's dare to let fear have its reign, and it didn't work out the way he'd hoped, not by a long shot. He climbed aboard a ship heading to Tarshish and in direct disobedience, fled the presence of the Lord. He boarded the ship, promptly went down into the lowest part, and fell into a deep sleep. Meanwhile, a great storm began to violently toss the ship. The fierce storm chased Jonah, because God had chosen him to go to Nineveh and *go he would*, by hook or by crook.

The terrified sailors cast lots to see who was responsible for the violent storm, and of course the lot fell to Jonah. Jonah knew perfectly well he was the cause of the storm, so he directed the frightened men to throw him into the raging sea, certain it would calm down once he was out of the boat. He might have been terrified to go to Nineveh but at least he took responsibility for the storm.

The sailors tossed Jonah overboard and the raging waves calmed, causing the sailors to fear the Lord, offer a sacrifice, and take vows. Hmmm. . .is it possible our disobedience can cause others to acknowledge the Lord? These heathen sailors offered a sacrifice to Jonah's God and took vows once they threw him overboard and saw the storm stop. I love how his disobedience caused a mini revival to break out among the sailors!

"Now the LORD had prepared a great fish to swallow Jonah. And Jonah was in the belly of the fish three days and three nights" (Jonah 1:17). I don't know exactly what kind of fish the Lord prepared, but I know God can fashion any kind of critter He sees fit to make. So, I imagine it was a gigantic whale, but who knows? No matter what kind of fish God made, he swallowed Jonah whole, not to consume him but to protect him and take him to Nineveh. God's grace is amazing, I get it, but sometimes His grace is absolutely terrifying!

Can you even imagine being in the belly of a gigantic sea creature—the odors, the heat, the warm intestinal juices all over your body? Oh, my word. I. Can't. Even. Yet Jonah survived. How he survived, I don't know, but God does. And Jonah prayed. He worshipped inside the belly of the fish, and I love how Matthew Henry puts it: "Many will not be brought to prayer till they are frightened to it; he that would learn to pray, let him go to sea."[9]

Ain't *that* the truth!

After three days in its belly, the fish vomited Jonah onto the dry land. The word of the Lord came to Jonah a *second* time, and this time he had enough sense to obey. "Now the word of the LORD came to Jonah the second time, saying, 'Arise, go to Nineveh, that great city, and preach to it the message that I tell you.' So Jonah arose and went to Nineveh, according to the word of the LORD. Now Nineveh was an exceedingly great city, a three-day journey in extent. And Jonah began to enter the city on the first day's walk. Then he cried out and said, 'Yet forty days, and Nineveh shall be overthrown!'" (Jonah 3:1–4).

In Hebrew, those words, "Yet forty days, and Nineveh shall be overthrown" are a mere five words. Five little words preached by Jonah completely changed the destiny of a nation. . .for a century and a half! God knew the Assyrians were ready, even if Jonah didn't.

> So the people of Nineveh believed God, proclaimed a fast, and put on sackcloth, from the greatest to the least of them. Then word came to the king of Nineveh; and he arose from his throne and laid aside his robe, covered himself with sackcloth and sat in ashes. And he caused it to be proclaimed and published throughout Nineveh by the decree of the king and his nobles, saying,
>
> > Let neither man nor beast, herd nor flock, taste anything; do not let them eat, or drink water. But let man and beast be

---

[9] Matthew Henry, *Matthew Henry's Commentary on the Whole Bible: Volume IV–IV Joel to Malachi* (Woodstock, Ontario: Devoted Publishing, 2017), 79.

covered with sackcloth, and cry mightily to God; yes, let every
one turn from his evil way and from the violence that is in
his hands. Who can tell if God will turn and relent, and turn
away from His fierce anger, so that we may not perish?

Then God saw their works, that they turned from their
evil way; and God relented from the disaster that He had
said He would bring upon them, and He did not do it.
(Jonah 3:5–10)

So what does Jonah do at this miraculous turn of events? Does he prostrate himself and celebrate and praise his God? No. Cranky Jonah gets ticked off in a big way. He's profoundly angry at God's mercy, so angry in fact, he asked God to take his life. Can you imagine being so invidious at God's mercy for your enemy that you would rather *die* than see them repent? It's actually almost comic. But our great God has compassion on *all* the nations of the earth. We are told to love our enemies, to forgive those who sin against us—and that right there may be one of the most difficult God Dares of all.

God presents Jonah and all of us with a deep question at the end of the story: "And should I not pity Nineveh, that great city, in which are more than one hundred and twenty thousand persons who cannot discern between their right hand and their left—and much livestock?" (Jonah 4:11).

Are we not to pity those living in treacherous nations who don't know the Lord? What if God called *you* to go? Would you? Or would you run in the opposite direction like Jonah, desperately attempting to flee from His presence?

Jonah had a misconception of God. His idea of God, a God of justice, mercy, and truth, caused him to mistakenly believe he had every right to hate the Assyrians and not go to Nineveh. He forgot God's true nature includes love and compassion. We can never let our *idea* of God get in the way of our obedience. Jonah acted in his own strength, and it nearly killed him. God's vision is the *only* vision that matters.

Scriptures to Think About

- *"The men of Nineveh will rise up in the judgment with this generation and condemn it, for they repented at the preaching of Jonah; and indeed a greater than Jonah is here."* (Luke 11:32)
- *"A gracious God and merciful, slow to anger and abounding in steadfast love."* (Jonah 4:2 ESV)
- *"And should I not pity Nineveh, that great city, in which are more than one hundred and twenty thousand persons who cannot discern between their right hand and their left—and much livestock?"* (Jonah 4:11)

God Dare Secrets

- Sometimes God will dare us to do a life-threatening thing—the direct opposite of what common sense and conventional wisdom would tell us to do.
- The God Dare always exposes what's in our hearts.
- God's grace can be terrifying in its manifestation in our lives.
- Never let your idea of God get in the way of your obedience.
- God will test each of us with a Nineveh at some point in our lives.

Discussion Questions

- Has God ever asked you to do something you didn't want to do? How did that end up?

- If God asks you to preach salvation to your enemies, will you go?

- Will you set aside your prejudice to bring repentance to a nation or a people group you don't like if God calls you to go?

- What's your Nineveh? Are you running from it or to it?

- Are you willing to embrace the calling on your life?

- What God Dare are you rejecting because of fear?

Chapter 16

THE DEVIL'S DARE

Be sober-minded; be watchful. Your adversary the devil prowls
around like a roaring lion, seeking someone to devour.
1 PETER 5:8 ESV

The devil and Jesus both have a plan for your life and be certain of this: *you* choose which one you listen to. When you say yes to the God Dare, hell takes notice! You'll need to fight hard for your dream before it becomes reality. The enemy of your soul hovers around your life, your dreams, your God Dare—and he will devour them in a heartbeat if he gets the slightest opportunity. He will try to seduce you and then loudly accuse when you fall into his demonic trap.

Your enemies? Most dwell deep in your mind and they're the usual suspects: fear, worry, pride, procrastination, laziness, distraction, the tyranny of the urgent, impatience, doubt, unbelief, worldly mindedness, cynicism, perfectionism, offense, and materialism.

It is amazing how quickly these enemies rear their ugly heads when their domains are threatened by your dreams. The truth is your enemies are dream killers and dream thieves. . .hindrances to your God Dare. And the vast majority of the time they are birthed in the mind. Our thoughts are where it *all* begins:

For though we walk in the flesh, we do not war according to
the flesh. For the weapons of our warfare are not carnal but
mighty in God for pulling down strongholds, casting down

arguments and every high thing that exalts itself against the knowledge of God, bringing every thought into captivity to the obedience of Christ, and being ready to punish all disobedience when your obedience is fulfilled. (2 Corinthians 10:3–6)

The enemy's goal is to make whatever we face so big, so impossible, so daunting it obscures the "knowledge of God." The devil does not want us to know God because he is well aware, the better we know God the more clearly we can spot his demonic trap.

He is a liar and the father of lies, yet his voice screams incredibly loud and relentless in our ears, daring us to doubt and tempting unbelief. If we let him, he will feed our fear, ignore our excuses, and gleefully provide us new ones. He is the king of defeat, depression, doubt, and distraction. When fear, greed, and self-justification saturate our brains, it comes *straight* from the pit of hell.

Where the God Dare is faith, love, courage, hope, and belief, the devil's dare is doubt, pride, lust, fear, and temptation. The consequences of taking the devil's dare are myriad, causing us to fall into sin, anger, depression, and murder, to name just a few.

Doubt and Pride

What is weapon number one in the enemy's arsenal, the very first one he used against humanity? *Doubt.* It's still his absolute best weapon. "Has God *really* said?" he'll gently whisper. "Are you *sure* you heard Him?" And my personal favorite, "Really, Kate, are you serious? Who do you think you are? What qualifies *you*? Why would anyone listen to anything *you* say? What makes you think you have a prayer at success?"

Thoughts are definitely things, and as the Word of God reminds us: "For as he thinks in his heart, so is he" (Proverbs 23:7).

I've rephrased it to go like this: we will become what we think about most of the time. The antidote? "Take every thought captive to obey Christ" (2 Corinthians 10:5 ESV).

If you've heard your God Dare, hopefully by now you've prayed through, counted the cost, and are eager to begin. Now doubt begins its evil, pernicious drumbeat in the back of your mind. Thoughts pound, and you realize maybe you bit off more than you can chew, maybe you're not equipped, and maybe you're losing your mind and never heard God at all! More than anything else, doubt will cause us to question God.

Stop right there! Examine those thoughts, and speak this out loud: "I can do all things through [Christ] who strengthens me" (Philippians 4:13).

Remember, He dared you knowing full well you couldn't accomplish it without His help. You are not alone!

What God revealed to you on the mountaintop—the flash of inspiration, the dream, the clear call—you now take with you into real life. You're going to work out your God Dare in the day-to-day when there's no beautiful music, when inspiration is but a distant memory, and you get little notice or praise. Obscurity is one of God's favorite training grounds.

How do you overcome the evil voice of doubt? Speak God's truth over your life. Talk to a trusted spiritual mentor. Put on praise and worship music. Pray. Review your God Dare. But whatever you do, Do. Not. Quit!

Adam and Eve

Adam and Eve were the first humans to hear Satan's nasty, wicked dare, and because he's cunning and quiet, they never saw him coming. Satan is a smooth operator, and he'll place a little seed of doubt in your mind with the goal of getting you to question your beliefs, your plans, your values, in fact everything you think you know.

The devil's dare always starts with a simple question: Has God *really* said what you think He said? The best example is the very first question in the Bible: "Has God indeed said, 'You shall not eat of every tree of the garden'?" (Genesis 3:1).

See what he did there? His simple question caused Eve to use logic and reasoning, getting her to think about the one thing God forbade her to have. His true goal? Make her want something she didn't even know she wanted. The devil brilliantly created an unmet need in Eve, a need for something she never knew she needed because she already had everything! He used charm and logic to make her think God didn't really love her. And his evil plan worked—and it still works today! The devil will use whatever he can to make us feel dissatisfied with what we have.

> *And the woman said to the serpent, "We may eat the fruit of the trees of the garden; but of the fruit of the tree which is in the midst of the garden, God has said, 'You shall not eat it, nor shall you touch it, lest you die.'" Then the serpent said to the woman, "You will not surely die. For God knows that in the day you eat of it your eyes will be opened, and you will be like God, knowing good and evil."* (Genesis 3:2–5)

God is keeping something good from you, Eve! Can't you see it? Something to make you *just like God*.

Satan first questioned what God actually said, sprinkled in doubt, and as his boldness grew, he called God a liar and stoked the fires of pride. He perverted what God commanded Eve, suggesting God's admonitions were not true.

Eve attributed three qualities to the tree:

1. She saw the tree was good for food.
2. She saw it was pleasant to look at.

3. She recognized it had the ability to make her wise.

And Eve added one more thing God never even said—"nor shall you touch it"—after doubt was injected into her heart.

There was one additional attribute even more critical than these: In eating of the tree she would be like God! How could God keep that from her? I mean, why *shouldn't* she be equal to God? Why shouldn't she be the hero of her own story? Pride rose up and Eve wanted to do what she wanted to do. God was no longer the boss of her—what could possibly go wrong?

What's the fruit of all this talk about fruit? Using the devil's logic, Eve saw no harm in taking a bite. Logic trumped obedience and reason trounced faith. When the enemy of our souls dangled his sweet bait in her face, she bit, and then Adam did as well. Eve was deceived, but Adam directly disobeyed God's strict command. Adam sat there listening to this whole conversation. Why didn't he interject and try to stop the craziness? Only God knows. As soon as they bit into the fruit, they discovered to their horror the devil's truth was a huge lie, but by then it was far too late. The rest is our unfortunate human history.

Throughout the next two chapters, I will share seven "spiritual secrets" I've discovered as I've pursued my own God Dares.

Spiritual Secret # 1: Pray God's promises.

It's a good practice to remind God and ourselves of His Word. I'm a big believer in praying His Word out loud and putting my name right there in the scripture. God instructs us to come boldly before the throne of grace, to bring Him our petitions, to ASK: **a**sk, **s**eek, **k**nock. Doing so ignites your God Dare and inspires your faith more than anything else. Do this even on the days when you might think you aren't making any progress. If you could see into the spiritual realm, you would see just how effective you are and how heaven is buzzing on your behalf. But for His own reasons, God doesn't give us that glimpse. Instead He requires we walk by faith and not by sight and instructs us to call "those things which do not exist as though they did" (Romans 4:17).

Cain

Cain was next in line to fall for the devil's dare. Adam's rebellion and disobedience allowed sin to enter the human race, planting the seed of murder into the heart of Adam's firstborn son, Cain.

Adam and Eve had two sons: Abel who kept sheep and Cain who tilled the ground. Both brought an offering to the Lord. Abel's offering was accepted, perhaps because it really cost him something since he had to sacrifice an animal. But Cain's sacrifice, which came from the ground God had cursed, was not accepted. God rejected Cain's offering, which mightily ticked Cain off.

So God questioned Cain and asked him why he was angry. He reminds Cain if he does well, he'll be accepted, but if he doesn't, sin is crouching behind the door waiting to pounce. Cain's job is to control himself and rule over sin, but sadly we all know how this story ends. Cain murdered his brother in cold blood, and when God asked him where his brother was, Cain spoke the first lie recorded in the Bible: "I do not know. Am I my brother's keeper?" (Genesis 4:9).

Sin began its hostile takeover in Cain's life as self-pity turned to jealousy, jealousy to hate, and hate morphed into murder, the ultimate end of the devil's dare. Cain ends up being sentenced by God to become a wanderer and vagabond on the earth. "The thief does not come except to steal, and to kill, and to destroy. I have come that they may have life, and that they may have it more abundantly" (John 10:10).

Lot and His Wife

When we meddle and try to pick what we want, making things happen our way, the outcome can be disastrous. Remember what happened to Lot in the book of Genesis? Lot and Abraham have to choose which land to move to, because the land couldn't sustain them both: "Now the land was not able to support them, that they might dwell together, for their possessions were so great that they could not dwell together" (Genesis 13:6).

So Abraham graciously allows Lot to choose first, but instead of inquiring of the Lord, Lot simply chooses the better-looking land, the "well-watered plain" as it says in Genesis 13. Lot didn't realize in picking the pretty land he was picking Sodom, a place destined to destruction by God. He didn't know when he made his fateful choice he would barely escape with his life, lose his wife, end up fathering two children with his daughters, and cause strife between two nations that still affects the world today. He chose to pitch his tent toward Sodom, a move that nearly costs him his life, in spite of it being well known that the men of Sodom were "exceedingly wicked and sinful against the LORD" (Genesis 13:13).

Contrast Lot's fate with Abraham, who, in letting Lot choose first and trusting God to pick *for* him, inherited God's promise of the land being given to him and his seed *forever*! A promise still standing today! When we're not wholly submitted to God it can end up causing all kinds of trouble for us.

How often do we make God over into our own preferred image of someone who does things our way, clearing all obstacles, showering down blessings, giving us great options, and letting us pick the one we like the best. Wouldn't it be nice if it worked that way? As much as we wish it were so, God will not be pushed around until He hands us the future we'd like. He is the sovereign God of the universe, and He alone knows exactly what we need.

If you're familiar with the story, you remember how Lot's wife looked back. Her heart, deeply wedded to the awful city where sin abounded, caused her to make a life-altering choice. Her entire being was wrapped up there, and possibly believing the angel's command didn't include her, she looked back at the burning city and in that instant, turned into a pillar of salt.

Esau

Esau just makes me cringe, and I'm amazed every time I read his story. How on earth do you give away your birthright and the double portion of the inheritance, the position of the firstborn and all its blessings, for a simple pot of stew! I don't get it. I've been hungry and experienced low blood sugar, but I have a hard time understanding it—unless Esau didn't really value what he had, or maybe he thought he would one day regain his position. Clearly, he didn't know his brother very well, because Jacob was one crafty sibling.

The way I understand it, the birthright was Esau's because he was the firstborn. But scripture tells us Jacob had the *promise*. God spoke to Rebekah when she was pregnant with twins Esau and Jacob, "Two nations are in your womb, and two peoples from within you will be separated; one people will be stronger than the other, and the older will serve the younger" (Genesis 25:23 NIV).

Rebekah was carrying two distinctly different individuals, twins but not identical in any way. Two people groups were represented: one who would value the world and all its pleasures and one who would (eventually) value God and the things of the Spirit.

God instructs Rebekah that Jacob, the second born, will be first, the one from whom the Messiah will come. Jacob began to desire first place and, not willing to wait for God's plan to unfold, attempted to manipulate circumstances by dishonest means and his mother's help. Had they let God bring it about in His timing, they would have saved much suffering in their lives and the history of God's people. But at least Jacob grasped the importance of the birthright. Esau despised it.

Esau treated great privilege with disdain, and the Bible labels him *profane* because of it. Esau sold out to the world, his own flesh, and the temptations of the devil, and though, like Judas, he felt remorse and regretted it later, he never repented. Remorse is NOT repentance. It's interesting to note Esau lost his birthright when he returned, famished, from a day of hunting, and he lost his inheritance when he went out to hunt, an activity he dearly loved. Good is often the enemy of the best, and sadly, Esau never got his blessing back.

Spiritual Secret #2: Don't let offense, unforgiveness, bitterness, jealousy, resentment, or anything else derail your God Dare.

Do the opposite of what the enemy is trying to convince you to do. When he wants you to hold on to offense, let it go and forgive, and instead, serve the ones who have mistreated you. Like the Beatitudes teach us—bless those who curse you, pray for those who despitefully use you. I heard this phrase years ago, and it's how I like to think of it: *Kiss the stones that bloodied your feet.* It's one of the hardest things we'll ever do, but it will transform our relationship with the one who gave His life for us. I learned this the hard way and I'm here to tell you, there is no other way to learn how to "pray for those who despitefully use you" until you've been despitefully used!

Fear

When I am afraid, I put my trust in you.
PSALM 56:3–4 ESV

Fear is a liar and the evil, hissing twin of doubt. It will always tell you why you can't or shouldn't do something. Fear is a lying spirit, and the only way to battle fear is to do exactly the opposite of what it says. Fear is that nasty voice in your head trying desperately to convince you why you should not do what God is calling you to do as it lays bare every obstacle. . .all the while reminding you of your impotence. Fear will massage your excuses and then throw you more. Fear stops you from growing and gives you every sensible reason *not* to. In fact, fear is a basic and primitive emotion, and any decision we make based in fear isn't really a decision at all. It's a *reaction*.

We can choose to listen or not. We alone get to decide if fear is the voice we want to hear. Fear is a choice every single time, and it's the polar opposite of faith. An acronym we've all heard is fear is "False Evidence Appearing Real." To reach out and contact someone you don't know well and ask for help is scary. Saying yes to a big opportunity is scary. Walking out of your comfort zone is scary. Sitting down at the keyboard to write your hard story is scary. Moving halfway around the world to become a missionary is scary. Saying no to the good in order to have the best is scary. Taking the lower place when you know you deserve the higher one is scary. Trusting God when you can't see the outcome is scary. Letting Jesus pick your future is scary.

When God prepared the Israelites to cross into the promised land, He flat out told them they would have to fight to possess it. Repeatedly He told Joshua, *"Be strong and of good courage,"* because God knew what He was asking him to do would terrify any normal person. God knew if Joshua looked at the circumstances he would be tempted to fear. The Israelites were about to inherit a land flowing with milk and honey, but they weren't going to receive it without a struggle and a battle. They were required to fight and dispossess nations bigger and mightier than themselves to walk into their destiny. God let them know on their own it wasn't remotely possible, but with God, we know *all* things are possible. "And we know that all things work together for good to those who love God, to those who are the called according to His purpose" (Romans 8:28).

Fear and anxiety will become our constant companions if we let them, so we'll need to be willing to do something really hard, something I used to tell my daughter when she was younger and being called out of her comfort zone more and more. I learned it big-time the first night I went on as the leading lady in *The King and I*.

"Do it afraid. But do it."

There is one good thing about fear. If you're afraid, be assured you're likely on the right track and you're moving from decision to destiny. Fear wants more than anything else to keep you *exactly* where you are, comfortable and safe. When it creeps in, know you're moving from complacency directly into your future. One piece of advice from me to you: don't let someone who may be scared to face their own God Dare talk you out of yours.

You know the feeling that hits when you're driving in your car and suddenly a dog runs out in front of you so you slam on the brakes to avoid hitting it? That panicked dump of cortisol that hits your stomach with the "fight or flight" feeling? Okay, now just imagine that feeling not going away. Constant waves of fear and anxiety, eating into your soul and spirit every moment of every day. That was my life for months, and it scared the living daylights out of me. Maybe that was the point.

Fear paralyzes. It stops you from being able to do *anything* productive, even eat. In fact, I lost five pounds in one week but not in a good way. I literally had no appetite and had to force myself to eat, but absolutely *nothing* tasted good. I know the enemy tried his best to stop me from writing what I needed to write, saying what I needed to say, teaching what I needed to teach, and doing what I needed to do. He took his best shot, but the Lord has sustained me through it all.

I'm learning that the enemy doesn't come to steal what I don't have. He's after my future, and he's after yours too. I've learned a lot in the last few years. Honestly, not lessons I wanted to learn but lessons I *needed* to learn. If we're going to go on with God, to grow deeply in our understanding of His ways, He'll begin to entrust us with suffering, with sorrow, with pain.

For me, it manifested as crippling anxiety. If you've ever dealt with it, you know exactly what I'm talking about, and if you haven't, no amount of explaining will help. In the midst of it, I made a big mistake. I got hooked on a prescription medication, Xanax to be precise. Now if you're taking something for anxiety, believe me, there is no judgment here—I know what you're dealing with, and I know how quickly relief can come with a pill. But for me, after a year of taking the lowest dose, I began experiencing frightening things. Every now and then I would wake up and honestly not know where I was or what I'd done the day before.

Once, in a huge hotel in New York City, I found myself wandering the halls in the middle of the night in a waking dream. Thank God He led me back to our room (it was a BIG hotel), and I knocked on the door and my husband, utterly perplexed, let me in. After that, whenever we traveled, he would block the door to our room with a chair so I couldn't get out and wander all over a strange hotel.

Xanax affected my memory as well. There are still moments from the last few years I can't recall. But in the spring of 2017 our lives settled down. I weaned myself off the Xanax and I've been drug-free ever since. It's hard, but it's not impossible.

During the worst of my anxiety, I begged God to take it away. He didn't for quite some time, because in His wisdom, He trusted me with His silence. When God trusts you with silence, it means

He knows you can handle a deeper revelation about His purpose. You thought He was giving you a stone, but you find He is giving you the Bread of Life. His silence proves you can handle the deeper deeps.

For those of you not experiencing anxiety, breathe deep and enjoy the mountaintop. For those of you in the valley, look up and remember the mountaintop. And breathe. . .deep. Enjoy the mountaintop, but know you're going to live out what you learn down in the "demon-possessed valley." Because the valley is where real life happens. The valley draws you close, makes you strong, shows you who He really is. And more importantly, who YOU are. The valley separates the men from the boys. The ones who'll pay the price to go deep versus the ones content to stay on the surface.

God did not promise life without struggle. Victory comes through battle, and triumph only follows trial. Sometimes God will take away what we want in order to test us. When Paul said, "We felt that we had received the sentence of death. But that was to make us rely not on ourselves but on God who raises the dead" (2 Corinthians 1:9 ESV), Paul knew God's purpose was good. Paul learned to trust Him more than life, to delight in Him more than in his own strength. The Bible doesn't say we will never fear. But it does tell us what to do when fear attacks: "Whenever I am afraid, I will trust in You" (Psalm 56:3).

I think sometimes God will break you in order to remake you. For me, what helped was repenting of anything and everything I could think of (mostly holding judgment and needing to release it), forgiving anyone and everyone as far back as I could remember, and building myself up by speaking truth over my life. Remember, *faith comes by hearing*, so don't hesitate to speak God's truth over yourself.

Here is the truth: fear is our enemy. I've always believed you need to do the exact opposite of what fear tells you to do. If fear tells you to run, stand your ground. If fear tells you to cower, smack it in the face. If fear tells you to be quiet, shout louder!

Through it all God has taught me powerful lessons:

- God will unravel to reveal.
- He will disorder to reorder.
- He doesn't want my self-sufficiency but only God-sufficiency.
- Fear is a liar.

Don't you just love the Proverbs 31 woman? She is everything I admire, but one of the things I love most about her is this: "She is clothed with strength and dignity; she can laugh at the days to come" (Proverbs 31:25 NIV).

I'm doing much better these days. Lots of prayer, thanksgiving, worship, and laughing at the future are helping tremendously, along with clean eating and avoiding toxins. I still have the occasional hard day, but they are few and far between. If you're dealing with fear or anxiety, keep trusting, hold tight to the One who knows your name. Trust in His goodness, and know His plans for you are good.

How do we fight fear? With three main weapons: prayer, praise, and thanksgiving. Determine today to break up with fear!

Prayer

You know by now we never take the God Dare alone. It's His dare, so let God help you! Make prayer your holy habit every day; don't start your tasks without it. Involve Him in your day-to-day decisions. God is a God of the details. Know that He deeply cares about even the smallest matters, so involve Him in every decision. Memorize scriptures to help you. In His forty days in the wilderness, Jesus fought Satan with three little words: "It is written." It is still our best strategy and strongest weapon. "For the word of God is living and powerful, and sharper than any two-edged sword, piercing even to the division of soul and spirit, and of joints and marrow, and is a discerner of the thoughts and intents of the heart" (Hebrews 4:12).

We know prayer changes circumstances, but more than anything, prayer changes *us*. Prayer gives us God's perspective, fills us with faith, and partners us with God to allow His purposes (and our God Dare) to come to pass. Nothing trumps prayer in the life of a believer. I've absolutely *clung to* this scripture the past eighteen months: "Be anxious for nothing, but in everything by prayer and supplication, with thanksgiving, let your requests be made known to God; and the peace of God, which surpasses all understanding, will guard your hearts and minds through Christ Jesus" (Philippians 4:6–7).

When God says be anxious for nothing, He means *nothing*! When you're no longer anxious, you'll find it easier to truly pray with thanksgiving

Praise

Enter his gates with thanksgiving and his courts with praise.
PSALM 100:4 NIV

When we praise God we acknowledge all His wonderful attributes. We remind ourselves over and over how big, how grand and glorious, how real our God is. We go from "us-centered" to "God-centered." As we list and reflect on His attributes and give God the glory, we put ourselves in the posture of humility, and we're reminded He is God and we are not. Our minds are washed clean; our spirits are renewed. We gain God's perspective and see things from His place, which is high above our earthly problems, yet deeply involved in all our affairs. Praise takes the focus off *us* and leads organically to the next weapon in our arsenal.

Thanksgiving

As we pray and speak God's words back to Him, we can't help but praise Him for His goodness. As we meditate on His attributes, we naturally begin to ponder His work in fashioning our destiny. The longer we walk with Him, the more we can look back and see His history of faithfulness in our own lives.

We thank God for life and breath and any of a million everyday details. The enemy loves to bring doubt and fear and will do all he can to make us think either God's passed over us, doesn't like us, is punishing us, or some other rotten nugget of twisted theology. The enemy loves to get us so wound up and self-absorbed, all we can do is wallow in self-pity and be of no use to the kingdom.

Thanksgiving is critical, but it's hard to get there when you're not getting what you want so badly. I've had to check my attitude many, many times in the last two years! (Waiting can reveal a whole lot of ugly, I promise.) Gratitude knocks self-pity out of the park and knocks the devil right on his backside! We gain God's perspective, and when we thank Him, we see things from His vantage point. We see the glorious, beautiful truth in these scriptures:

- *God is love.* (1 John 4:8)
- *Every good gift and every perfect gift is from above, and comes down from the Father of lights, with whom there is no variation or shadow of turning.* (James 1:17)
- *"For I know the plans I have for you," declares the LORD, "plans to prosper you and not to harm you, plans to give you hope and a future."* (Jeremiah 29:11 NIV)

Spiritual Secret #3: Anointing is costly.

God told Paul he would suffer for his faith, and we know how very deeply he did. The enemy will oppose you at every turn because he will oppose anything and everything God breathes life into and calls important. There will be a cost, I guarantee it, but if you are steadfast, your life will yield something beautiful—*fruit*.

The Twelve Spies

These twelve guys drive me nuts, y'all. They are like the Greek chorus of negativity in all our lives. They are the dream-stealers, the deafening voices of fear and doubt shouting lies in our heads, telling us why we can't, won't, or shouldn't do what God is calling us to do. All they can see are the giants, yet they miss the ginormous grapes! Grapes so big they need two men to carry one cluster! Can you even *imagine* grapes like that? Yes, there were giants. . . but there were giant grapes too! "Then they came to the Valley of Eshcol, and there cut down a branch with one cluster of grapes; they carried it between two of them on a pole" (Numbers 13:23).

Doubt and fear are powerful negative motivators that can stop a God Dare in its tracks and delay it for years. Often they come at us from those who know us well and believe they have our best interests at heart. They see the obstacles but not the promise.

In Numbers 13, God instructs Moses to spy out the promised land of Canaan by sending one man from each of the twelve tribes of Israel. So the twelve head out to see what the land, the people, the cities, and forests are like. They go to spy out the land and see that it's good, *really* good, and fruitful. When they come to the Valley of Eshcol, they find those amazing giant-size grapes, and in fact cut some down to bring back with them.

Here's how it all plays out. The twelve spies return from the land and report that it really *does* flow with milk and honey, and yes indeed it is a good land. But, they tell Moses, the people are strong, the cities are fortified and huge, and the inhabitants are descendants of Anak, a race of giants. In fact, they say they are like grasshoppers compared to the descendants of Anak. They report that the Canaanites dwell there, with firm belief it's impossible to overcome them. All they can see are the hindrances, causing them to ignore God's incredible promises. They see giants and miss the giant fruit. They see the impossible and refuse to allow God to ignite the possible.

A Bad Report of a Good Land

In fact, they give a *bad* report of a *good* land. Sure, there were giants, and I'm sure giants are frightening and hard to kill, and probably have bad breath, but they forgot the main thing: *they had God on their side.* He had already brought them out of Egypt, parted the Red Sea, brought water out of the rock, fed them daily with manna from heaven, and guarded their camp with a pillar of fire by night and a pillar of cloud by day. He'd done all those incredible, miraculous acts, yet *still* they doubted.

Now, we all have doubts and taking the God Dare can be scary, I grant you. But regret is far worse, and oh, how those Israelites lived to regret their decision to give in to fear. Not one single person of that entire generation over twenty years old lived to see the promised land. *Not one.* Millions died in the desert and only two, Joshua and Caleb, went in to occupy the promised land because they were the only two who had true courage and believed in their futures enough to fight for them.

Spiritual Secret #4: Just do it!

If you've discerned that now is the time, then step out. Have courage and do the thing God is calling you to do. James 2 admonishes us to add works to our faith. If God has given you the go-ahead, it's disobedience to wait. Stepping out into your God Dare takes courage, but you can do ALL things through Christ who gives you strength.

Those Who Took Both Dares

I think Sarai/Sarah sometimes gets a bad rap. She did what was considered acceptable in her culture, like give her maid to her husband to have a baby. Admittedly, God had spoken to Abraham and promised *him* much, and she was to be part of it all, but the years were clicking by and no baby was anywhere on the horizon. She did what she felt she had to do. And at that time period in history, any baby born by her maid automatically became hers. So, I get it. Sarah was trying to work it out in her own strength. And because she listened to doubt rather than faith, she gave in. Why am I not surprised that Abraham hardly protested at all when she offered him Hagar, her young maid?

Sarah ended up with the baby she wanted but unwittingly created a rivalry between two brothers and people groups that negatively affected the world in ugly ways thousands of years later. Sarah had to choose between trusting the flesh or trusting the Spirit, and she chose the former. "It is the Spirit who gives life; the flesh profits nothing. The words that I speak to you are spirit, and they are life" (John 6:63).

Eventually she got it right and gave birth to her own child at ninety years old! She's included in the book of Hebrews' hall of faith: "By faith Sarah herself also received strength to conceive seed, and she bore a child when she was past the age, because she judged Him faithful who had promised" (Hebrews 11:11).

King David is another who took both dares. His remarkable faith in God allowed him to slay Goliath with nothing but a sling and a stone (talk about a God Dare!). Years later, after becoming king of Israel, the snare of lust lured him into grave sin and he seduced Bathsheba, another man's wife. She becomes pregnant; he has her husband killed and takes her as his wife. In spite of this sad and sinful episode, what we remember about David is this: he was a man after God's own heart. We remember the good in his life and hopefully learn from the bad.

Solomon took both dares; as did Saul who became Paul, Peter the rock, and many more. Most of us, no, *all of us* have taken the devil's dare to doubt or fear at one time or another. It's just human nature. Thankfully, it's not how we start but how we finish!

Scriptures to Think About

- *Lest there be any fornicator or profane person like Esau, who for one morsel of food sold his birthright. For you know that afterward, when he wanted to inherit the blessing, he was rejected, for he found no place for repentance, though he sought it diligently with tears.* (Hebrews 12:16–17)

- *Every good gift and every perfect gift is from above, and comes down from the Father of lights, with whom there is no variation or shadow of turning.* (James 1:17)

- *"For I know the plans I have for you," declares the* LORD, *"plans to prosper you and not to harm you, plans to give you hope and a future."* (Jeremiah 29:11 NIV)

- *"It is the Spirit who gives life; the flesh profits nothing. The words that I speak to you are spirit, and they are life."* (John 6:63)

God Dare Secrets

- Sometimes, the thing we love most can blind us to what we have that's best.
- There are people around us who will steal our God Dare right out of our hands and hearts.
- Be careful what voices you listen to. Some will feed your fear, and some will feed your faith.
- Good is often the enemy of the best.

Discussion Questions

- How has the good become the enemy of the best in your life?

- Is someone holding your God Dare hostage because they're giving a bad report of a good land? What can you do to set your God Dare free from their grasp?

- Can you look back to a time when you took both the God Dare and the devil's dare? What did that look like?

- What doubts are letting you see only the giants and missing the giant grapes?

- What are you waiting for before you begin pursuing your God Dare? Are you waiting to begin until circumstances are just right?

- Do you believe the sins of your past have disqualified you from being used by God? How so?

Chapter 17

GOD DARE ENEMIES

The enemy comes to steal, kill, and destroy your God Dare; and in these modern times we're living in, we afford him loads of unique opportunities to accomplish his dastardly goals. This chapter reveals some of his favorite weapons of mass destruction.

Distraction

Some of you will set your faces like flint and conquer your God Dare with relentless precision in record time. The rest of us will get started with enthusiasm and energy until weariness begins to set in and inspiration fades. This is the moment distraction makes its grand entrance.

The internet is an amazing invention, but rife with pitfalls and time wasters. Like a siren's song, Facebook and Instagram call our names. Twitter, email, video games, and Pinterest fairly beg for our attention. For me, simply sitting at my computer and seeing unread emails pulls me from my set goal for the day and leads me down a circuitous path, wasting my time at a remarkable rate. A comment on Facebook I really must respond to, a request for a recipe I simply can't ignore, ooh, a sale at my favorite online store that ends today. . .and on and on it goes as the time flies by.

I've become ruthless with social media and online distraction because if I'm not, these distractions will ruthlessly upend my God Dare. There are only twenty-four hours in each day, and I know that how we spend them will determine our futures. Thankfully, we don't have to unplug completely, but we do need to set online limits.

The internet is aptly named the World Wide Web, because like a spider's web it can trap us and suck the life right out of us. My advice: be vigilant with social media and time spent online. Delete all you can, unsubscribe to the time-wasting blogs and online stores, and set a timer to limit your online scrolling. Your God Dare will bear eternal fruit; your time on social media won't. Interruptions happen, and it's your call whether to invite them in or not. If you do invite them in, don't allow them to get you off track and keep you off track for the whole day. Jump back in as soon as you're able.

If you do work at home, you'll need to schedule work and family times so when it's time to be with your family you can be fully engaged with them and not resent being taken away from pursuing your God Dare. Maybe God dared you to finish your college degree. You'll need time to study and time to go to class. It's all about balance! Talk with your family members and come up with a plan you can all live with. Enough unforeseen things will occur. . .the three-year-old throws a tantrum at breakfast, the dishwasher breaks, the car battery dies. . .to pull you away from your task. Schedules help.

I procrastinate on the important things that grow bigger and loom larger with each passing day. If I neglect them for too long, well, that's when the crazy kicks in. Let's say you've neglected to pay the bills or file your taxes on time and you suddenly realize your mistake. Now you're in a panic, pressed for time, forced to scramble and reshuffle your entire schedule for something that was utterly avoidable.

The Tyranny of the Urgent

The *urgent* suddenly trumps the *important,* causing you to lose ground. Often, the urgent appears because we've neglected something back when it was small and likely annoying (um. . .paying bills). Everything else gets pushed to the side until the urgent task is taken care of. My advice? Plan your days, make lists, delegate wherever possible, and schedule time to review your progress weekly. Do what you can to stay ahead of the game!

The tyranny of the urgent is a sneaky and subtle thief, snatching our God Dare right out from under us. The urgent creates stress and lets chaos rule our day, stealing our time, our sanity, and our money. . .especially if we've neglected paying bills or haven't attended to those minor home repairs that, if left too long, cause major headaches.

Change is the norm in our lives now, and most of us in the Western world are on information overload. Social media and twenty-four-hour cable news alerts pull and tug at our time and attention. It's a daily fight to stay ahead of the game and out of the traps, to ignore all the extraneous voices pleading for our time, attention, and money.

Everything is **BOLD AND IN CAPS! SHOUTING TO BE HEARD OVER ALL THE OTHER NOISE!**

It's so loud it can easily drown out the still, small voice of your God Dare, buried under all the noise. "We live in constant tension between the urgent and the important. The problem is that the important task rarely must be done today or even this week. . . . But the urgent tasks call for instant action—endless demands; pressure every hour and day."[10]

Look back at the goals for your God Dare, and look honestly at your life and the basic tasks needing to be done each day/week/month. Determine what's important. Paying bills on time is important. Not paying them on time makes the task urgent. Do you homeschool your kids? If so, planning your curriculum and lessons is important. Not planning leads to chaos. What's important in

---

[10] Charles E. Hummel, *The Tyranny of the Urgent* (Chicago: Inter-Varsity Christian Fellowship of the United States of America, 1967).

your family? Make a list and you'll come up with your important tasks. This will help you avoid turning them into the urgent.

We can expect the unexpected to rush headlong into our lives, requiring an urgent response. Have you ever gotten in your car in the morning to head to an appointment only to find a dead battery or a flat tire? Or had a child run a fever just as you got him or her ready for school? What about when your dishwasher breaks moments before company rings the doorbell? Or when any one of the million things that *can* go wrong *does* go wrong? All of us have to deal with the urgent from time to time. . .it's just part of life.

What we don't want is to let neglect, procrastination, laziness, distraction, or fear dictate our actions. Because if they do, our dreams become derailed. We can't control everything, but we can control many things. On the plus side, we'll have more time to move our God Dare forward. We all need to accept this truth: "In this world you will have trouble. But take heart! I have overcome the world" (John 16:33 NIV).

Enemy Attacks

Let's talk turkey here. When you take the God Dare, you have a target on your back. The devil hates you and will do all he can to throw you off track and derail your God Dare, using his favorite weapons of fear and doubt, distraction and laziness, the tyranny of the urgent—*anything* that he can use to find a chink in your armor.

Let me risk getting all up in your business for a minute. "As he thinketh in his heart, so is he" (Proverbs 23:7 KJV). It all begins in the mind. Thoughts are things, and how we *think* determines how we *live*. Our thoughts will affect every area of our lives.

Satan loves to attack the mind. It's how he first dealt with humans back in the Garden of Eden. By asking a simple, innocent-sounding question about fruit, he sowed evil seeds of doubt into Eve's mind, causing her to focus on the tree of the knowledge of good and evil. How could a good God withhold something so amazing, something to make her wise and something to make her *like* God? In the end, she bit. Thoughts turned to disobedient actions that brought down the entire human race. It's Satan's go-to tactic, and he uses it just as much today as he did then. He will use it on you too, I guarantee it.

Guard your mind! Take exquisite care what you allow to influence your thoughts. We are to "cast down" wrong thoughts and "vain imaginations" and bring them into captivity for this reason: we will become what we think about!

- *As he thinketh in his heart, so is he.* (Proverbs 23:7 KJV)
- *And do not be conformed to this world, but be transformed by the renewing of your mind, that you may prove what is that good and acceptable and perfect will of God.* (Romans 12:2)
- *Jesus said to him, "If you can believe, all things are possible to him who believes."* (Mark 9:23)

This is the key to the God Dare. . .it all starts in the mind! If you *believe* it, then you'll *see* it. How do you do this? What is this mysterious mind-transforming trick? Three activities have worked for me: prayer, scripture memory, and taking extreme care with what I allow to invade my mind. As Christians, one of our most precious treasures is possessing the mind of Christ in all its diverse beauty and rich creativity.

First Corinthians 2:16 says, "But we have the mind of Christ."

And we're reminded in Colossians 3:16, "Let the word of Christ dwell in you richly."

Hide His Word in your heart!

"Your word I have hidden in my heart, that I might not sin against You" (Psalm 119:11).

There are an abundance of wonderful scripture memory apps

and programs available. Find one you like and use it. Nothing will renew your mind and purify your heart like meditating on God's holy and transforming Word.

So, what should we allow in? How do we decipher the good from the bad, the holy from the profane? One of my life scriptures is this one from Philippians:

> *Finally, brethren, whatever things are true, whatever things are noble, whatever things are just, whatever things are pure, whatever things are lovely, whatever things are of good report, if there is any virtue and if there is anything praiseworthy— meditate on these things.* (Philippians 4:8)

These ancient words have become my plumb line. Everything I watch, read, or listen to must be held up to this standard to see where it falls and where I might fail. The TV shows and movies I watch, the music on my playlist, the books I read, my web surfing—are they noble and pure and lovely? Is there any virtue in them? It makes a difference. You've heard the expression, "Garbage in, garbage out"? It's never truer than what we allow in our minds.

In the last twenty years there has been an information explosion in this world. The book of Daniel warns us, "Knowledge shall increase," and knowledge continues to increase day by day. Any and every ungodly thing, subject, sin, distraction, and desecration are available at the mere touch of a button. There are many dangerous doorways. Our friends in Hollywood and the media are in business to make money, and they've learned well that sin sells. They're not invested in your well-being and don't care a whit about helping you guard your heart and pursue your God Dare.

Be careful and prayerful about the media you and your family consume. . .*especially* your children. Your mind is a precious possession, your body the temple of the Holy Spirit. If Jesus were to pick up your iPhone or Kindle right now or take a gander at your search history or what's on your DVR or iPad, would He be pleased? It's black and white, my friend; there are no shades of gray. Take great care what you allow to invade your temple—your God Dare depends on it. " 'All things are lawful for me,' but not all things are helpful. 'All things are lawful for me,' but I will not be dominated by anything" (1 Corinthians 6:12 ESV).

Laziness and Procrastination

I know all about this one—in fact, I would consider myself a *professional* at procrastination. It's way too easy for me to put off till tomorrow what I really should do today. My husband calls me the "excuse queen" because I can justify just about anything. I have a dozen reasons why I simply can't work on my manuscript today. They're usually plausible and good-sounding excuses, but they don't hold water. We all have the same time to spend each day, but how we choose to fill our God-given time on earth separates the men from the boys or those willing to do what it takes from those who aren't. Twenty years from now you'll be way more disappointed by the things you *didn't* do than by the things you did.

If I sincerely believe God has tasked me with something important He wants me to do, then for me at least, I believe it's a sin to procrastinate and not get to it. To procrastinate is the equivalent of taking my God Dare and throwing it back in God's face, telling the Creator of the universe the task He's appointed for me isn't important enough to do today, right now. Possibly you're procrastinating because you're stuck in a rut and inspiration is fading. Or maybe your God Dare is causing you to face things in your life or your past, scary things you really don't want to revisit or think about.

Has God dared you to write or speak about dark times or difficult experiences that cause bad memories of the past to surface? Fear can cause us to put things off so long we never face them at all. My advice? If at its core your procrastination is not laziness but fear…then pray, dear one. God is faithful to show you and help you through the pain and the memories as He strengthens you for the task. Remember, your God Dare is not about *you*—its purpose is to change lives. "For God has not given us a spirit of fear, but of power and of love and of a sound mind" (2 Timothy 1:7).

Remember a few pages back when we discussed fear being a lying spirit and the importance of doing the opposite of what it tells us? Yeah, *that*. You will have to fight. We must go face-to-face with it because if we're not vigilant in this, fear will paralyze us. The worse our fear, or in my case, crippling anxiety, the more powerful and the more necessary our obedience becomes because our overcoming story will change lives.

On the other hand, maybe you've given laziness a place. Maybe you're one who has always let things slide, yet have always gotten by. Sorry to tell you, my friend, it's not going to cut it with your God Dare! To accomplish your dare, you need to be resolute, unflinching, determined, and diligent. There are many scriptures warning against laziness and many praising diligence and hard work. Here are a few to ponder.

- *He who has a slack hand becomes poor, but the hand of the diligent makes rich.* (Proverbs 10:4)
- *The soul of the sluggard craves and gets nothing, while the soul of the diligent is richly supplied.* (Proverbs 13:4 ESV)
- *He who is slothful in his work is a brother to him who is a great destroyer.* (Proverbs 18:9)
- *Therefore, my beloved brethren, be steadfast, immovable, always abounding in the work of the Lord, knowing that your toil is not in vain in the Lord.* (1 Corinthians 15:58)

This is one of my favorite scriptures, and it's all about the destiny of the diligent:

Do you see a man who excels in his work? He will stand before kings; he will not stand before unknown men. (Proverbs 22:29)

If laziness or procrastination is your deal, get with God and repent. Laziness is sin, and only through repentance can we move beyond it and make progress. Maybe it's a generational curse needing to be broken, maybe it's pride. Pray, and the Lord will show you. For me it's usually self-indulgence, me saying my agenda is more important than God's.

Whatever it is, unless you're ruthless, it will stop your God Dare in its tracks. That would be a shame because, hear me now, if God has dared you, then we need whatever it is He's dared you to do! We all have our places in His plan, and yours is just as important as everyone else's. Start today. Pray, repent, receive forgiveness, and get ruthless with your excuses.

Spiritual Secret #5: Be patient.

Some God Dares take years; others are accomplished much more quickly. The slow ones take focus and determination beyond what we're innately capable of. When things are moving slowly for me, like they have been through the writing of much of this book, there's one scripture I go back to again and again: "But those who wait on the LORD shall renew their strength; they shall mount up with wings like eagles, they shall run and not be weary, they shall walk and not faint" (Isaiah 40:31).

I desperately need my strength renewed daily, don't you? I long for eagles' wings. I want to run and not grow weary. I long to walk and not grow faint, but I will only accomplish my goal as I wait upon the Lord, His timing, His way, His decision.

Abraham and Sarah waited twenty-five years for their promise to come to pass. Joseph had to endure thirteen years of slavery and prison. Moses waited in the desert for forty years. Forty! Your God Dare may not happen quickly. It may take years before you see fruit. Is it worth the wait? You tell me. If God has clearly instructed you to take action, is it your place to say no? To tell the Creator of the universe that what He's created you for is taking too long? Just because you may not see anything happening, heaven is working on your behalf. Sometimes, God simply needs to set certain things in motion in our lives, and we may not necessarily know what they are. If you know God has called you, are you willing to wait, like Abraham? Hang in there, friend, and know He's in your future setting everything up.

Worldly-Mindedness

Will you do what it takes to be *extra*ordinary? Are you willing to persevere, to set your face like flint, to not give in to the enemy called "average"? Are you willing to go against the flow, the popular opinion, and the well-intentioned but poorly reasoned advice to do what others refuse to do? Are you willing to take and finish your God Dare, and be the change the world so desperately needs?

The Land of Good Enough is where most people live their lives and raise their children and families. Fear, laziness, procrastination, materialism, and unbelief stop many from leaving any positive legacy or impact at all. They raise their children, keeping the bar low, neither expecting nor requiring excellence from themselves or anybody else and unfortunately, they get *exactly* what they expect. My husband often reminds me when I'm frustrated by inefficiency or bad service that the world is run by C students and unfortunately, he's right.

It's all related to what we believe about ourselves. All throughout her childhood, I continued to remind my daughter she was a world-changer. I told her God thought she was extraordinary and that He had an incredible life planned for her from before the foundation of the world. I spoke God's truth over her, and her accomplishments have proved His words true. My husband and I set the bar high. We expected excellence and did our best to model its pursuit in our own lives. We weren't perfect parents by any stretch, but we established a model of behavior she could follow because we understood this truth: children will believe whatever you tell them about themselves. So, speak life. Speak truth. Speak *destiny* over your children.

God tells us He's already prepared work for us to do. He has good works with your name on them just waiting for you to begin. This scripture is the God Dare spelled out: "For we are His workmanship, created in Christ Jesus for good works, which God prepared beforehand that we should walk in them" (Ephesians 2:10).

I didn't learn these precious truths growing up and, as a result, floundered aimlessly for years. Once I became a Christian and began to study the Word, I uncovered the truth of how God sees me. I learned I'm

- Fearfully and wonderfully made
- God's workmanship, created for good works
- Written on the palms of His hands
- Not condemned, even though I deserve it
- The righteousness of God in Christ Jesus
- Set free in Christ
- Blessed with every spiritual blessing in the heavenly places

These are just a few—there are a thousand more. I speak these truths over you. Speak them over yourself and your children out loud! His Word never returns void, and it will absolutely change your life and renew your mind.

Spiritual Secret #6: Press in to know Him.

As you pursue your God Dare, maintain a deepening relationship with Christ. Keep it at the forefront as your primary goal. To gain your God Dare yet grow distant from God is tragic. Keep the main thing the main thing, and I promise you, *Jesus is the main thing*.

Comparison and Competition

My husband says men are from Google and women are from Pinterest! I love Pinterest, but looking at it usually makes me feel like a complete failure. Everything is so perfect and I just don't measure up. My house will never be so cleverly decorated or efficiently organized. I'm not crafty, and though I pin lots of DIY with the best of intentions, I can tell you honestly I will likely never actually follow through and make *any* of those things.

Worse yet, if I allow myself, I'm easily intimidated by most of the authors and bloggers I follow. Their writing is expressive and beautiful, they take gorgeous photos for their blogs, have way more followers than I do—tribes, even—so I might as well just throw in the towel, right?

That's exactly what the enemy would like me to do. He would love nothing more than to intimidate me right out of my God Dare. If I compare myself with other writers and bloggers, I'll be found wanting every time. The devil wants me to listen to the voices of insecurity and doubt already lurking in my subconscious. He wants me to pull them out and turn up the volume on their accusations. "Who do you think you are, Kate? You're not gifted enough, smart enough, young enough, connected enough, or educated enough to pull this off. You're not fooling anybody. You might as well just give up before you're utterly embarrassed!"

Please don't listen! If God has called you, then He knows *exactly* what He's doing, and He will equip you for the task. Maybe part of your miracle and testimony is the fact that you *are* small and unknown. If you're gifted enough, smart enough, connected enough, young enough (or old enough), and educated enough, what on earth do you need God for?

The whole point of the God Dare is to believe in the impossible, walk by faith and not by sight, and take God at His word in complete trust. Your obedience will impact the ones it will impact. Do numbers matter to you? Popularity? Beating the competition? If I let my numbers dictate my God Dare, then I would stop writing today. But God has shown me this little nugget of truth.

We All Have Our Spheres

I have a circle of lives I impact with my life and words and blog posts, and you have a circle completely different from mine. Likely I won't reach your circle and you might not reach mine. But each of us has something unique and important to contribute. We all do our part.

> *From whom the whole body, joined and knit together by what* **every joint supplies,** *according to the effective working by which* **every part does its share,** *causes growth of the body for the edifying of itself in love.* (Ephesians 4:16, emphasis added)

Whether I'm called to reach two hundred or two million, in the infamous words of a former presidential candidate: "What difference does it make?"[11] The point is not my reach compared to yours; the point is obedience. We sow in faith and let God give the increase as He sees fit.

If popularity or numbers or fame or fortune is what drives you, you might need to take a good hard look inside and make sure it's

---

[11] "SEN BENGHAZI HRG: CLINTON," https://www.youtube.com/watch?v=F66mGV8x-Kqo, posted by CNN, July 21, 2016.

God's Dare you're following. Not that some God Dares don't lead to those things, but honestly, not always. Most of us will labor in obscurity, but if God has dared you, no God Dare is too small that it can't change the world. Trust me, fame is not all it's cracked up to be. My sweet daughter can tell you it's rarely glamorous, it's a huge responsibility, and it's hard, hard work to maintain.

You have a unique voice in all the world, a singular calling, a distinct destiny. God created you for it, and it really doesn't matter how you compare with someone else. Just like Jesus told Peter after the resurrection, when he was all worked up about what Jesus was calling John to do. With an uncompromising answer, Jesus gently put Peter firmly in his place with these words: "If I will that he remain till I come, what is that to you? You follow Me" (John 21:22).

He's saying the same to you and me today. "*You* follow *Me*." Don't compare and don't look longingly at another's path. You have no idea the price they've paid for their God Dare.

Perfectionism

You're not perfect and you never will be, and that's okay. In all of history there's only been one perfect person, and He was crucified because of it. If you struggle with perfectionism you might have a harder time with your God Dare. Here are a few reasons why.

- You will think you have to wait until circumstances are perfect before you can begin.
- You will want to control every detail and every outcome.
- You are by nature risk-averse, and you'll take the God Dare only if you're certain you will succeed.
- You are terrified to fail, so fear will try to paralyze you and stop your God Dare before it starts.
- Your standards are high, and you'll do *anything* to avoid an average or mediocre outcome.

- Setbacks will smack you down and prove you're not good enough.

Perfectionism is quite different from striving for excellence. If you make a mistake when striving for excellence, you'll just work a little harder because you don't view a mistake as something wrong with you. Perfectionists, on the other hand, mistakenly learned early in life that value was rooted in achievement. You were only as good as what you *did*. Your life is all about the "*shoulds*."

Here's the good news: perfectionism is a learned behavior, and not an inherited trait. Chances are you learned early on your value was based on what you accomplished. Love and affirmation had to be earned and weren't given easily. Perfectionism is the polar opposite of grace, and grace can never be earned because it's a free gift! "Being confident of this very thing, that He who has begun a good work in you will complete it until the day of Jesus Christ" (Philippians 1:6).

Did you catch that? *He* does the work! The *good* work! Weakness is the perfectionists' worst enemy, yet Paul boasted in his! "And He said to me, 'My grace is sufficient for you, for My strength is made perfect in weakness.' Therefore, most gladly I will rather boast in my infirmities, that the power of Christ may rest upon me. . . . For when I am weak, then I am strong" (2 Corinthians 12:9–10).

Today's Grace

We only get enough grace for today. We can't store it up till tomorrow and we can't depend on yesterday's. Today's grace is the only grace we have. And if I'm not careful, I'll miss today's grace. Each day I have choices to make about the grace in my life.

- I can manufacture grace or manifest it into a life of love.
- I can ignore grace or invite it to indwell my heart.

- I can deny grace or deliver it to others every day.
- I can try to understand grace or undertake to know the One who gives it with an open and generous hand.

Every day Jesus teaches me to abide in grace, reminding me His yoke is easy, His burden light. My burdens weigh me down, stifle the life, crush dreams, fill my heavy heart with guilt. But He whispers that He adores me, everything about me—the good, the bad, and the ugly. And as you've already read, there's plenty of ugly. His death on the cross wasn't for the perfect me. It was for the sin-soaked me. The rebellious me. The imperfect me where sin dwells in spite of my best efforts.

My imperfect life is where His grace is released and begins its perfect work. Slowly, daily, fashioning my heart into the woman of God He created me to be. He takes me as I am and shows me a little more of who He is each day.

He is not what I thought He was at the beginning. He's most definitely not the Christian art print Jesus, all smiles and meek, carrying a lamb on His shoulders, tan and blow-dried, with perfect teeth and bright blue eyes. A matinee-idol Jesus. No, He's definitely not that.

He's strange and strong; resolute and remarkable; odd and off-putting; and far, far ahead of me with His face set like flint. I do my utmost to follow His fading footprints, wherever they lead. Some days I run, mostly I walk, and many days my victory is in simply standing. Because sin unceasingly reminds me that it dwells in me. But grace shouts: Jesus loves every bit of every atom that He created! I can only put one foot ahead of the other, take one day at a time, pick up my cross and be willing to die *today*.

Friend, the truth is, He loves every bit of you. He loves the frustrations and the failures, the tragedies and triumphs of your life. The sweat and the struggle. The hurt and the hollow, all the empty parts. The imperfect and the ugly. Because you're fearfully and wonderfully made by Him. In fact, *you* are worth dying for.

You didn't earn His grace, and it will never, ever make sense. It's grace, and I can't even scratch the surface of all it means. But that's okay. I don't need to fully understand it; I just need to receive it and walk it out *today*. So let His words ring in your spirit as you grasp His amazing grace.

> *But he said to me, "My grace is sufficient for you, for my power is made perfect in weakness." Therefore, I will boast all the more gladly of my weaknesses, so that the power of Christ may rest upon me.* (2 Corinthians 12:9 ESV)

The Pharisees kept all their laws and traditions perfectly, avoiding anything unclean, not accepting imperfection from anyone, yet when the Perfect came, they were too blind to recognize the true Son of God, so they rejected Jesus, having Him brutally murdered. Newsflash! None of us can ever be good enough. Nothing we do can earn His love because we already have it.

If you struggle with perfectionism, there are a few things you can do to help.

- Face your fears. What's the worst thing that can happen? Seriously, what is it?
- Mistakes are how we grow. What can you learn from yours?
- There's more to life than what you *do*. Sometimes you just need to *be*.
- The journey you're on is just as important as the destination.

Perfectionism is a demonic trap, a lie and an illusion. Your worth in God's eyes is not by what you do. Did you know He chose you in Him before the foundation of the world, before you ever did anything? Salvation can't be earned! Don't let perfectionism derail your God Dare. Pray, repent, and ask God to help you conquer this most treacherous impediment to your dream.

Self-Pity

We all have what I like to call our "favorite bad feeling," the place we go first when the unforeseen obstacle careens into our path. Mine is self-pity. I'm pretty sure it comes from being the middle child of four siblings, the third born, but second of three girls and always feeling passed over and/or left out. I didn't have the privileged position of either the firstborn girl or the baby so I always felt unnoticed and stuck in the middle. You could've just painted a bull's-eye on my back and said, "Here, devil, drop self-pity right here!"

When something happens in my life I don't like, can't control, or can't wrap my brain around, I typically resort to wallowing, "woe is me" and all that. Neither God-honoring nor mature, but when you're in the midst of a pity-party, the mud seems a perfectly fit place to hang out. God will allow me to wallow for only so long until He uses something or someone, usually my husband, to snap me out of it. As soon as I get out of the mud puddle and choose gratitude, the most amazing thing happens: my self-pity lifts and I begin to see the devil's hand. "Yet in all these things we are more than conquerors through Him who loved us" (Romans 8:37).

Oswald Chambers says it like this:

What does it matter if external circumstances are hard? Why should they not be! If we give way to self-pity and indulge in the luxury of misery, we banish God's riches from our own lives and hinder others from entering into His provision. No sin is worse than the sin of self-pity, because it obliterates God and puts self-interest upon the throne. It opens our mouths to spit out murmurings and our lives become craving spiritual sponges, there is nothing lovely or generous about them.[12]

The enemy enjoys keeping me down and depressed, morose, and moaning, hardly the stance of a warrior ready to do battle and emerge victorious. It's easy to forget, but please remember, we've already won the battle! Our perspective needs to shift.

Perception and Perspective

I always get a window seat when I fly. Always. I love looking out the window, far above the clouds where all the people and all my problems shrink to tiny specks. I get a new perspective every time I'm in the air, and I realize the truth of my position. Above. I'm learning life is all about perception and perspective.

Perception, what you see and how you see it, is your reality. It's not necessarily truth but it's *your* truth. Only one thing can change your perception and that's your perspective, the place you look at life from. We go through life dragging our heavy burdens behind us, the chains of our misconceptions birthed in wrong perceptions. We drag around our version of truth, except it's not truth; it's our perception of truth.

Our carnal minds think, *It's not fair, I got a raw deal, I have no purpose, I'm of little value, My sin has disqualified me, I'm too old, I'm still single*, etc. We sit and complain, wallow and moan, and we'll stay there unless our perspective shifts. Paul reminds us of our true position: "God raised us up with Christ and seated us with him in the heavenly realms in Christ Jesus" (Ephesians 2:6 NIV). "Therefore, if anyone is in Christ, he is a new creation; old things have passed away; behold, all things have become new" (2 Corinthians 5:17).

When we know our position, where we really, truly are, we gain a new perspective, and our perception shifts from lies to

---

[12] Oswald Chambers, *My Utmost for His Highest*, May 16.

truth. What loomed large suddenly shrinks, like those specks on the ground, because our true position as believers is this: we are above everything *He* is above. We are seated where He is seated, above what He is above, and we have His authority over everything we're above—and we're above everything! Above fear, guilt, shame, depression, self-pity, perfectionism, bitterness, offense, jealousies, comparisons, accusations, anxiety, the lies of the enemy—above anything and everything dragging us down into the mud.

We see ourselves earth-bound, weighted down with insurmountable problems, yet He sees us risen above, sitting with Him, at rest and at peace. Oh, what a glorious thing to consider! Isn't it time we stopped inviting our past to determine our future? To remember His will for us is blessing, abundant life, and victory? Isn't it time to stop seeing our lives as merely a battlefield filled with depression, fear, shame, guilt, and rejection? Isn't it time to be overcomers and more than conquerors? Yes, it's a battle, but I'm here to remind you, we win!

Our mind is the front line of our faith, and we're only changed as we renew our minds. In fact, Paul says we're transformed. We are changed, remodeled, transfigured, reconstructed! We become like Him as we behold His truth and let go of ours. It's time to change our mind-set from fear to faith. Our lives will transform when we let the pain of the past and fear of the future quit infecting all the potential of our present.

Guilt and Shame

Guilt and shame are simply this: *toxic*. We've all been exposed at some point, and God is the only One who can get the poison out of our system. All of us have junk in our pasts, broken places we don't want exposed, and many of us feel disqualified from ever being used by God *because* of our past sins. I know for sure I did. I couldn't imagine a holy God using my unholy life to change the world. Guilt and shame about my abortion nearly overwhelmed me for decades.

But God.

Jesus said five life-altering words to the woman caught in adultery: "*Go and sin no more.*" He dared me and He dares you with those same words today. If you've repented of your sin, you're forgiven, and you can use your experience to bring healing to someone else. Guilt and shame will cause us to miss our God Dare because they bring fear to join the party. We judge our worth, our fitness to take the God Dare by what we *see,* not by what He *says*:

"*I have chosen you.*"

"*I have redeemed you.*"

"*I love you with an everlasting love.*"

When we feel condemnation, He says, "There is now no condemnation" (Romans 8:1 NIV). When we compare ourselves and are found wanting, He says you are "fearfully and wonderfully made" (Psalm 139:14). When we see judgment, He says, "I will allure her, will bring her into the wilderness, and speak comfort to her" (Hosea 2:14).

I love this from Oswald Chambers:

Never be afraid when God brings back the past. Let memory have its way. It is a minister of God with its rebuke and chastisement and sorrow. God will turn the "might have been" into a wonderful culture for the future.[13]

God is the great restorer and redeemer! He will restore everything the devil has stolen from us. This great promise in Joel is one I hold close to my heart: "So I will restore to you the years that the swarming locust has eaten" (Joel 2:25).

---

[13] Oswald Chambers, *My Utmost for His Highest*, April 13.

Let me grab you by the shoulders, look you in the eyes, and tell you this: You're not disqualified. You're FORGIVEN! You're covered in His precious blood! You're a new creature! Don't get to the end of your life and look back in regret. Do the thing He's calling you to do, the hard, scary thing. Yes, it might expose your inner ugly, but when God shines His light, it transforms our failure into glorious triumph. It's costly to expose and reveal, but if He's calling you to it, it will cost you everything *not* to.

Spiritual Secret #7: Walk in unity and accountability with others.

Make sure you have a few folks you trust so you can get seasoned counsel and advice. Your mentor if you have one, your spouse if you're married, a trusted friend, and your pastor are all going to help keep you on the straight and narrow road. If you don't have a good Bible-teaching church, find one. When we lived in New Jersey, we made the long drive into Manhattan every Sunday to go to David Wilkerson's wonderful Times Square Church. Yes, it took more than an hour each way but as our friend reminded us, "The anointing is worth it!" Also, get good counsel from mature believers you trust and who will hold you accountable.

Scriptures to Think About

- *Trust in the LORD with all your heart, and lean not on your own understanding; in all your ways acknowledge Him, and He shall direct your paths.* (Proverbs 3:5–6)
- *For the weapons of our warfare are not carnal but mighty in God for pulling down strongholds.* (2 Corinthians 10:4)
- *Be sober-minded; be watchful. Your adversary the devil prowls around like a roaring lion, seeking someone to devour.* (1 Peter 5:8 ESV)
- *Take every thought captive to obey Christ.* (2 Corinthians 10:5 ESV)

- *Every good gift and every perfect gift is from above, and comes down from the Father of lights, with whom there is no variation or shadow of turning.* (James 1:17)
- *"For I know the plans I have for you," declares the LORD, "plans to prosper you and not to harm you, plans to give you hope and a future."* (Jeremiah 29:11 NIV)
- *Do you see a man who excels in his work? He will stand before kings; he will not stand before unknown men.* (Proverbs 22:29)

God Dare Secrets

- You can choose to stay safe. Or you can choose to be chosen and change the world.
- The only way to combat a trickle of doubt is with a flood of truth.
- Do it afraid, but do it.
- When you take the God Dare, hell takes notice.
- You can't control everything, but you *can* control many things.
- Obscurity is one of God's favorite training grounds.
- We will become what we think about!
- If God has called you, then He knows exactly what He's doing and He will equip you for the task.
- We are above everything He is above.
- You're not disqualified; you're forgiven!

Discussion Questions

- What's the biggest doubt or fear holding you back from saying yes to your God Dare?

- Are you willing to do it afraid? What does that look like?

- What's the biggest distraction to your God Dare? The biggest time-waster?

- How have you determined what's important in your life so it doesn't turn into the urgent?

- What are the enemy's favorite ways to attack your mind?

- What steps are you taking to be careful with what you allow into your mind?

- Are you comparing your God Dare with someone else's and feeling insecure? What can you do to combat that mind-set?

- What's your favorite bad feeling? Will you repent today?

- Will you wait patiently for your God Dare to come to pass?

Chapter 18

THE GREATEST GOD DARE OF ALL

Thick incense hangs sweet and heavy in the air as mysterious music resonates, thunderous and holy. The weight of glory nearly crushes the man as he worships, bowing him low to the ground. Prostrate, he catches a glimpse of something unearthly and glorious, frightening and awe-inspiring. In fact, a glimpse of glory weighs him down and the burden of his unrighteousness, his own filthy rags, presses and deeply convicts him of sin.

Isaiah's eyes catch a glimpse of the King of the universe for one brief, life-altering moment, and in that moment, the terrifying truth about himself penetrates his heart in a way he's never known. He realizes, much to his horror, he is *a man of unclean lips*" (Isaiah 6:5). The unvarnished truth sears him to the bone, and he can do nothing more than repent. Instantly, a seraphim, a burning one, touches a live coal to his lips, and forgiveness flows. Worship, repentance, and forgiveness open his ears, and clear as a bell he overhears the ancient, eternal question: "Whom shall I send, and who will go for Us?" (Isaiah 6:8).

What else could Isaiah answer when in the presence of God-of-the-Angel-Armies? "Here am I! Send me." So he volunteers to a future uncertain and an end unknown. He knows absolutely nothing about where he's to be sent, yet can't you see him practically throwing his hands up in the air and shouting, "Me! Pick me!! I'll go!!"

Who volunteers? Who will follow? Who's willing to be sent? Who will choose to be chosen?

Since eternity began, this same call has been ringing out, the divine question hanging over each of our lives for all of our lives, and our only decision is how we respond. All born-again believers are chosen, yet still we have a choice. We decide whether we hear and obey. It's completely up to us whether we follow or not. The call is for all of us, but God gives us free will, so it's our choice.

"Whom shall I send, and who will go for Us?" These ten words establish the destiny-defining question of the ages, echoing in the lives of the ones willing to go, to die, to speak, to live for God. Those willing to pay the price, those who *"love not their lives unto death."* The ones willing to lay down dreams and desires in order to see God's will done on earth as it is in heaven. These are the men and women who choose obscurity or fame, riches or poverty, the ends of the earth or hearth and home. They're the ones who hear and volunteer.

Isaiah was one. In repentance and forgiveness, he heard the God Dare way back in 740 BC; the dare to go into all the world and witness love and truth, justice and grace. We must become like Isaiah, knowing to the soles of our feet our unworthiness, yet receiving the free gift of acceptance, forgiveness, mercy, and grace with a heart willing to be sent.

Some of us are dared to glory, greatness, and high visibility. Most of us are dared to obscurity, living life in the small sphere, the family, the little town, the quiet yet world-changing life. God doesn't need us, but He values us deeply. The crucified thief took the God Dare to believe—proving it is never, ever too late. Can you be a nobody willing to exalt a Somebody?

Some of us are called to go, most are called to stay, but both can change the world if we follow because each of us has an assignment to alter our landscape. Each of us has been equipped with gifts and talents. It's up to us whether we decide to use them or let them lie fallow on the ground. The choice, as always, is ours.

"Blessed is that servant whom his master, when he comes, will find so doing." (Matthew 24:46)

It's a holy thing, this volunteering. We say yes and we wait to be sent. He sends us in *His* time, when the season is exactly right. They're the different ones, the ones who don't really fit in. They've heard something remarkable, and knowing they have nothing to offer but obedience, say, "I will" to the question of the ages: "Whom shall I send, and who will go for Us?"

Living in the Extraordinary Ordinary

There's no such thing as an ordinary life. Obscure? Indeed. Ordinary? No. I'm holding you by the shoulders and looking you in the eyes as I say this: *You are irreplaceable in God's story. Your words matter. Your life matters. YOU matter.*

I don't really care what you've done or how much you've messed up in your past—*you* are part of His story and *your life matters.*

"But I have ugly scars. God can't use me." You know what your scars are, my friend? They're badges of honor, proof of the battle. You may not have won every round, but your scars prove just this . . .*you were in the fight.*

You may want *big.* You may want purpose or impact. You may want numbers and a platform. Most of us want to be seen and heard. We all want our lives to matter. It's not essentially wrong; it's simply human. But it's not always the best.

What does living an extraordinary life mean to you? Think about your answer for a second. Is it multitudes hanging on your every word? Or maybe inventing something important or making a world-changing discovery? Is it being famous or fabulously wealthy? Having a best-selling book or a hit on the radio? A ministry or business impacting thousands?

All these pursuits can have a good purpose, but most of us will live our lives much more simply. We'll likely abide in the small sphere where tiny acts of obedience can still have a big impact. And where, ultimately, the big things often turn out to be tiny after all.

When Jesus took a towel and a basin of water and began washing His disciples' feet, it was a small act, but its impact still deeply moves us today and its example has changed the world and given us all a profound lesson of humility to follow.

As the sinful woman washed Jesus' feet with her tears and wiped them dry with her hair, her gesture seemed insignificant in the grand scheme of things, her act born of a love so profound it was all she knew to do. She didn't care a whit about recognition; she did it because she loved much. However, her impact turned out to be huge, and her stunning act of worship is celebrated two thousand years later.

Can I be honest with you? Most days I feel like an outsider to the grand Christian story. How on earth can *my* small, unimportant, obscure life cause even a *ripple* in the giant pond of history? How can *my* life have any significant impact?

Most of us live what the world would call "ordinary" lives. If we are following Christ, we do our best to obey God's commands and it's likely our lives go pretty much unnoticed. We don't feel like we're part of the "big story." Our lives aren't shaking nations, our platforms are small, we aren't evangelizing thousands, aren't selling millions of books. We feel left out, unimportant, obscure.

But please hear me. . .no matter how ordinary or insignificant you may think you are, your life matters. If you're living for Christ and making His name known in your sphere, then you're impacting the world in bigger ways than you can imagine. You count. And what you do counts too. Your life is critical to the story God is unfolding. Your living and teaching, your quiet serving and child-rearing, your giving and sacrificing, as small as they may seem, send out ripples. Be assured ripples can turn into tidal waves.

You are irreplaceable in God's story, and what you do matters. Your words matter. Your life matters.

YOU matter.

I'm all about the big God things, those moments when He stuns you with His future. I believe in big God Dares for you and your children. I adore how He brings a God Dare into your life and alters you forever. But the big God things take time. And sometimes, in our rush for big purpose, big ministry, big world-changing accomplishments, we can miss the small. The little. The insignificant.

We become so focused on the future, we miss *right now*. We forget an important truth:

Big lives are found in lots of small moments. Just as a symphony is thousands of little notes and a great painting filled with innumerable brushstrokes, our lives consist of millions of small but profound moments.

In fact, Jesus lived the biggest "small" life in history. He walked. He taught. He built. He wept. He ate. He healed. He laughed. He led. He cried. He loved. He found beauty in the small.

His big miracles can overshadow His small moments, but there's much His small moments teach us because they are saturated with holy significance. So many examples are in the Word when we search for the small.

Jesus Christ washed feet. He ate with Pharisees. He spent time at a well teaching one rejected woman about worship. He settled disagreements between disciples. He took time to bless children and ministered to a woman who sat at His feet. He paid taxes. He walked with the disciples. He prayed on a mountain. He went sailing. He cooked fish on a sandy seashore. He attended a wedding. He ate and drank with sinners and saints.

And in everything He did, He breathed on each small moment to teach us big lessons.

His ordinary moments still teach extraordinary truths today. He shows us how to live purposely, intentionally, steadily advancing toward the goal but not missing the journey.

Because small things make a big impact.

The touch of a hand, the encouraging phone call, making time for a friend, giving a hug. The handwritten note or basket of homemade muffins. The lullaby deep in the night, the car pools and housework, the teaching and training, the prayer or counsel lovingly shared. All small but significant. The little things we do absolutely change the world around us.

While waiting for the big, don't neglect the small. Follow His footsteps and find the beauty in the small in all the everyday moments. He'll show you the way.

Christ lived His life in the small sphere, but every small thing He did speaks to us today and continues to have an enormous impact.

Because Jesus Lived the Extraordinary Ordinary

He used mud and spit to bring sight to a blind man, bread and fish to feed thousands, a word and a touch to expel demons. Small acts that all had world-changing kingdom impact. We go to work each day and let our lives be a witness of grace, we raise our children to know and love the Lord, we volunteer to help the least of these, and we shine as lights in our communities, loving and serving with no expectations. And as we do that, we too can experience His extraordinary grace as we live the ordinary every day.

What extraordinary ordinary thing are you doing?

I don't know how God will Dare you. It might be something big—I can't possibly know. He says to each of us, *"Come to Me."* After you come to Him, set aside what you think you know and let Him speak to you. He will show you as you walk alongside Him. If you let Jesus pick, that's where you will find your life.

Is there a God Dare for the infertile woman? What about the fortysomething who's still unmarried? The unemployed man? The confused teen? The divorced dad? I'm convinced there is because ultimately the God Dare is to Jesus Christ Himself. Not to a nation or a cause, a belief or a passion, "but Christ is all and in all" (Colossians 3:11). It takes drastic obedience to follow God into your future.

The God Dare is the unexplainable effect of obedience. It's the end result of prayer manifested as service to the One who saved us from ourselves and from the ultimate goal of the enemy: eternity in hell. It's about our personal relationship to Christ, not our "usefulness" to the world.

God loved me long before I cared a whit about Him. He wrote my story eons before I was born. He wrote your story too, and He wrote it for a reason. Ephesians 2:10 says it like this: "For we are His workmanship, created in Christ Jesus for good works, which God prepared beforehand that we should walk in them."

Workmanship, *poiema* in the Greek, means "masterpiece." Do you realize you are God's masterpiece? Sit with that for a minute.

He has a plan in place for you, and He sees you according to how He created you, not by what you have or haven't done. Let the past stay there, and walk into the glorious future with Him.

The loudest human heart-cry is just this, to be enough, to know our lives matter, to believe we have purpose and significance, to understand we're here for a reason. To sense we're loved for who we are and not just because of what we've accomplished. Each of us has design and destiny in our DNA.

The God Dare answers the age-old question: Am I enough? When God dares you, He proves without a doubt. . .

Yes. You. Are.

You are because of a truth it's taken me a long while to fully understand. I'm enough because He is enough for me, and anything

He calls me to, He will equip me to do.

You are chosen by God.

Whatever He's daring you to do, you know up front you can't possibly accomplish it on your own because you're not strong enough. But then again, neither was Moses or Abraham. Esther wasn't either, or Rahab or Ruth, Job or Joseph. The God Dare lit a God-spark that spoke to their hearts, opened their ears, allowing them to discover their own God Dares, and in saying yes to God, each and every one of them changed the world.

But know this: the same God who commissioned Moses, comforted Hannah, spoke to Paul, called Abraham, and positioned Esther is speaking to *you* today. Let *that* sink in.

I'm praying as you read this book you'll sense your own God-spark and say yes to your God Dare. Because you *are* enough, and you're completely and utterly worth it. I'm praying my words will be a wake-up call to your heart.

> *"You did not choose me, but I chose you and appointed you that you should go and bear fruit and that your fruit should abide, so that whatever you ask the Father in my name, he may give it to you."* (John 15:16 ESV)

> *For we know, brothers and sisters loved by God, that he has chosen you.* (1 Thessalonians 1:4 NIV)

> *But you are a chosen race, a royal priesthood, a holy nation, a people for his own possession, that you may proclaim the excellencies of him who called you out of darkness into his marvelous light.* (1 Peter 2:9 ESV)

Isaiah was willing to go, to be sent, to do whatever God required of him. Who volunteers? Who will follow? Who's willing to be sent?

Who will choose to be chosen?

The question of the ages, the question that determines each of our destinies, is found in the New Testament. How we answer determines the trajectory of our lives and the success of our God Dare. Jesus asked it of His disciples, and He asks each of us the same exact question. First, He said, " 'Who do men say that I, the Son of Man, am?' So they said, 'Some say John the Baptist, some Elijah, and others Jeremiah or one of the prophets'" (Matthew 16:13–14).

Can't you just feel the pregnant pause, the obvious question hovering in the atmosphere? I consider what Jesus says next as *the most important question* in the Bible. I imagine Jesus looking each disciple in the eyes as He asks:

"*But who do* **you** *say that I am?*" (Matthew 16:15, emphasis added).

And bold Peter (my fave disciple) jumps right in with the correct answer, saying: "*You are the Christ, the Son of the living God*" (Matthew 16:16).

When we get the answer right, we're positioned by God to change the world. He is God and He gets to choose our futures, our God Dares, our everything. So now as we're nearing the end of this book, let me ask you a few questions.

Will You Let Jesus Pick?

Can Jesus help Himself to your life? Does He have permission to decide where you live, if you'll marry or have children, what you should study or do for a living? Does He get to pick poverty or riches, fame or obscurity? Are you okay if He allows a thorn in your flesh so His strength might be shown in your weakness? Will you go if He calls you out? Will you stay if He wants to plant you deep? Will you follow relentlessly, resisting the urge to look at another's path and be content with your own?

What if God dares you to give up your right to yourself, to

turn the other cheek, to be defrauded, to walk the second mile, to be reconciled to your brother? "In the history of God's work you will nearly always find that it has started from the obscure, the unknown, the ignored, but the steadfastly true to Jesus Christ."[14]

After more than thirty-five years of walking with the Lord, I know this about following: Jesus is in the business of making disciples.

> *"If anyone desires to come after Me, let him deny himself, and take up his cross, and follow Me."* (Matthew 16:24)

His way is the narrow way and because it's the way of the cross, there are few who find it. Do you want to be one of the few?

The call of God, the God Dare as I call it, constricts and constrains, leaving little wiggle room. It is what it is, different for each of us, and we can either take it or leave it. Who do *you* say He is? Is He bigger than your fear? Bigger than your pride? Bigger than what you think you deserve? Can He determine your destiny as He sees fit?

> *"You did not choose Me, but I chose you and appointed you that you should go and bear fruit, and that your fruit should remain."* (John 15:16)

> *"Many are called, but few are chosen."* (Matthew 22:14)

> *But you are a chosen generation.* (1 Peter 2:9)

Jesus Christ suffered and died for us. When we make Him Lord and Savior, we acknowledge His right to reign in our lives and circumstances. Jesus gets to pick.

---

[14] Oswald Chambers, *My Utmost for His Highest*, September 7.

I pray after reading this far you don't think you have to *do* something for God or have some burning desire to change the world. If you are burning, burn for *Him*, and let love be what burns and moves you. Most God Dares come suddenly, like Moses seeing a bush on fire in the distance. They come in the fullness of time when God is ready for us to step out and bungee jump into the future with Him.

Moses heard the God Dare in the desert, Abraham on a starry night, Joseph in the depths of a dream. It beckoned to Esther in the palace of a king, and through an angel to Mary of Nazareth. David heard it as he faced a giant, Rahab caught it in the voice of two spies, Ruth detected it in the sad voice of her mother-in-law, and John the Baptist heard it on death row. Peter, Paul, and James heard it clear as a bell, and it still calls out today.

The Greatest God Dare

He's asking you one simple question, the same one He asked me:

Am I enough?

He has an answer for that. The exact same answer He gave Moses centuries before in a barren desert by a burning bush.

"I AM."

His ways are not my ways, and the older I get the more I know it's true. He's pried open the box I'd carefully constructed for Him and slipped out, uncontainable, unboxable. He daily floods my soul with His truth, and the revelation strikes my heart that *He alone* knows exactly what I need and exactly *why* I was created.

The more I read the Bible, the more I'm convinced the God Dare saturates the vast landscape of scripture. You can sense it whispering from the mountaintop in its still, small voice as it drops deeply into the hearts of biblical heroes.

Can you hear it? Whispering in the summer wind, roaring in the waterfall, lingering in the raindrops, summoning your soul in its still, small voice. Daring you to believe. Imagine. Fight. Dream. Follow. Choose. *Say yes.*

What if you've read this far and you're thinking, *I don't think I have a God Dare. I don't think He's daring me to do anything big or important or risky for Him. I don't feel any sense of destiny about my life. I'm pretty sure God skipped right over me.* He hasn't! God doesn't call the qualified or the worthy. He calls the willing. He calls the ones who will hear and obey. Lots of small acts of obedience add up to a big, impactful life.

Precious one, let me let you in on a little secret I've saved until the end.

The biggest God dare of all is crystal clear: to live like Jesus. To really and truly bless when you are cursed, to love your enemies, to do good and pray for those who persecute and despitefully use you. To truly be the light of your world no matter how big or small your light may be. To forgive the ones who've deeply hurt you and release any offense still lingering.

To live your life willing to be broken bread and poured-out wine, to kiss the stones that bloodied your feet. To wash the feet of the ones who've betrayed and abandoned you and to let others help themselves to your life, whatever the cost. You may be called to do great things for God, but in the meantime be willing to wash feet. Wash, serve, give, and love while you wait.

This is the true test, to live like Christ. To lay down our lives, our agendas, our hopes and dreams, our ways and wants, our questions, our bodies, and to pick up our crosses and follow the One who showed us the way and daily teaches us how to walk.

The God Dare asks each of us to pick up our cross and follow Him. To obey whatever He tells us. To listen for His voice and then do what He says. To sprinkle holy salt and shine holy light on the people around us day after day. Whether it's in the boardroom or the laundry room, a worldwide platform or a homeschool classroom—

the setting isn't what's important. We don't change the world by *where* we are but by *whose* we are.

> *"Enter by the narrow gate; for wide is the gate and broad is*
> *the way that leads to destruction, and there are many who go*
> *in by it. Because narrow is the gate and difficult is the way*
> *which leads to life, and there are few who find it."*
> (Matthew 7:13–14)

You don't know when or how the God Dare will come or what age you'll be when it does. Your sole responsibility is to be ready when it arrives, and there's only one way I know to ready yourself. Get to know, deeply, the One who formed you, who chose you before the foundation of the world. The One who loves you so fiercely He was willing to die for you, the One who asks only one thing—that you live *like* Him and *for* Him.

Will you go like Abraham or lead like Moses? Will you risk your life like Esther or cling and follow like Ruth? Will you go against the flow like Rahab or risk looking foolish like Naaman? Will you dare to dream like Joseph or let God use tragedy in your life like Job? Will you say with Mary, "Be it unto me according to Your word. . ."?

Will *you* take the God Dare?

He will dare you with two of the simplest words you'll ever hear. The two words standing as pillars, as touchstones along the paths of our oh-so-different lives. Two words separating the sheep from the goats, the ones who take God at His word and believe it is worth *everything* to live a daring life, two simple words separating the ones who take the God Dare from the ones who refuse.

"Follow Me."

Jesus Christ's words in the beautiful, life-transforming Sermon on the Mount contain the seeds of the God Dare. You don't know where He'll take you, but wherever He goes is the absolute safest place to be. What is He daring *you* to do? Taking the God Dare changes everything.

"Blessed are the poor in spirit,
For theirs is the kingdom of heaven.
Blessed are those who mourn,
For they shall be comforted.
Blessed are the meek,
For they shall inherit the earth.
Blessed are those who hunger and thirst for righteousness,
For they shall be filled.
Blessed are the merciful,
For they shall obtain mercy.
Blessed are the pure in heart,
For they shall see God.
Blessed are the peacemakers,
For they shall be called sons of God.
Blessed are those who are persecuted for righteousness' sake,
For theirs is the kingdom of heaven." (Matthew 5:3–10)

To the amazing ones who are willing to press in and press through regardless of the circumstances, I sense the Lord standing there smiling, watching, hovering, and whispering to the angels:

"See those faithful ones, those precious saints of mine? All the burden on them yet still they worship, still they press on, still they love. I've seen their suffering and their obedience, their love and forgiveness, their hurt and their healing. I've heard every cry in the night and I've seen every single tear they have cried. In fact, no tear has been wasted—every single one has been captured in a bottle. I tested them deeply with My silence and still they loved, followed, and obeyed. I treasure their lives and I've

seen how they have treasured others and taken the lower place. I did not ever, for one second, leave or forsake them. I love each and every one of them, and though they may not be aware, the truth is, they have My entire heart and I know the steep price they've paid. I see. I know. And I stand in awe. . .wait till they see their crowns."

Scriptures to Think About

- *"Whom shall I send, and who will go for Us?"* (Isaiah 6:8)
- *"You did not choose Me, but I chose you and appointed you that you should go and bear fruit, and that your fruit should remain, that whatever you ask the Father in My name He may give you."* (John 15:16)
- *For we know, brothers loved by God, that he has chosen you.* (1 Thessalonians 1:4 ESV)
- *But you are a chosen race, a royal priesthood, a holy nation, a people for his own possession, that you may proclaim the excellencies of him who called you out of darkness into his marvelous light.* (1 Peter 2:9 ESV)
- *Then Jesus said to His disciples, "If anyone desires to come after Me, let him deny himself, and take up his cross, and follow Me. For whoever desires to save his life will lose it, but whoever loses his life for My sake will find it. For what profit is it to a man if he gains the whole world, and loses his own soul? Or what will a man give in exchange for his soul?"* (Matthew 16:24–26)

God Dare Secrets

- You are chosen by God.
- His way is the narrow way, and because it's the way of the cross, there are few who find it.
- The biggest God Dare of all is to live like Jesus.
- Taking the God Dare changes everything.
- The same power that raised Jesus from the dead is in *you*.
- Jesus gets to pick.

Discussion Questions

- What would change if God were to help Himself to your life?

- Does He get to pick what your God Dare looks like? Your destiny? How can you be sure?

- Are you willing to do what most won't do in order to have what most won't have?

- What steps are you taking to live your life like Jesus lived His?

- Will you follow Him wherever He leads?

- Will you take the narrow way?

RESOURCES FOR INFERTILITY,
ADOPTION, MISCARRIAGE,
AND ABORTION

Infertility and Adoption

Adopting After Infertility by Patricia Irwin Johnston
Surviving Infertility by Linda Salzer
Infertility: The Emotional Journey by Michelle Hanson
Labor of the Heart: A Parent's Guide to the Decisions and Emotions in Adoption by Kathleen Whitten

Books on Loss

Holding On to Hope by Nancy Guthrie
I'll Hold You in Heaven by Jack Hayford
Pastoral Care in Pregnancy Loss by Thomas Moe
Empty Cradle, Broken Heart: Surviving the Death of Your Baby by Deborah L. Davis
We Were Gonna Have a Baby But We Had an Angel Instead by Pat Schwiebert

Websites on Loss

www.mend.org
www.stillstandingmag.com
www.hannahshope.us

Abortion and Miscarriage

Grieving the Child I Never Knew by Kathe Wunnenberg

I'll Hold You in Heaven by Jack Hayford

A Season to Heal by Freed and Salazar

Save One by Sheila Harper

Project Rachel: www.hopeafterabortion.com

www.care-net.org

ABOUT THE AUTHOR

Kate Battistelli is an author, speaker, former actress/singer in the New York Broadway musical world, and mother of GRAMMY award-winning Contemporary Christian recording artist Francesca Battistelli. Kate's goal is to see you be all God has created you to be, and she truly believes each of us is here to change the world. It's how she raised her only child and it's her primary purpose in writing *The God Dare*.

She loves to speak about *The God Dare*, share *Bridging the Generation Gap* workshops in church and conference settings, and letting Jesus pick her future. She is a natural encourager and believes in your ability to change the world, even if you don't!

She recently moved to Franklin, Tennessee, to be closer to Francesca's growing family. She's been married to her husband, Mike, for thirty-four years and loves being near her daughter, son-in-law, and four amazing grandchildren.

IF YOU LIKED THIS BOOK,
YOU MAY ALSO LIKE...

Odd(ly) Enough
by Carolanne Miljavac

Social media star Carolanne Miljavac's *Odd(ly) Enough* is a message your heart needs to hear: It's time to embrace the "you" God made you to be. Tune out the naysayers of the world and jump into His loving arms. He'll walk alongside you as you passionately pursue your God-given purpose.
Paperback / 978-1-68322-789-2 / $14.99

Obedience Over Hustle
by Malinda Fuller

The world promises recognition and promotion if we "hustle harder," but the truth is that we seldom feel as though we can stop the chase. Join the countercultural movement of choosing *surrender* over striving alongside author Malinda Fuller, who encourages you to respond to the question God asks each of us: "Will you obey Me?"
Coming September 2019!
Paperback / 978-1-64352-075-9 / $14.99